Looking Back

Looking Back

Russell Baker

NEW YORK REVIEW BOOKS

New York

THIS IS A NEW YORK REVIEW BOOK

PUBLISHED BY THE NEW YORK REVIEW OF BOOKS

LOOKING BACK

by Russell Baker

Copyright © 2002 by NYREV, Inc.

This edition published in 2002
in the United States of America by
The New York Review of Books
1755 Broadway
New York, NY 10019
www.nybooks.com

Library of Congress Cataloging-in-Publication Data

Baker, Russell, 1925–
    Looking back / by Russell Baker.
        p. cm.
    ISBN1-59017-008-3 (hardcover : alk. paper)
    1. United States — Biography. 2. Biography — 20th century. I. Title.
CT220 .B24 2002
973.9'092'2 — dc21

                                                        2002000748

ISBN 1-59017-008-3

Printed in the United States of America on acid-free paper.

April 2002

for James M. Cannon

Contents

Introduction

This book contains a number of men who were or desperately wanted to be president of the United States. It is tempting to say that all who want that office want it desperately, but such is not the case. Barry Goldwater and Eugene Debs are notable exceptions to the desperado rule, and they mingle here, like gentlemen fallen among brutes, with such ferocious strivers as Theodore Roosevelt, William Randolph Hearst, Richard Nixon, Lyndon Johnson, and the Kennedy brothers John and Robert.

Franklin Roosevelt also appears here briefly, infuriating Hearst with a soak-the-rich tax bill aimed straight at Hearst's bank account, then having the gall to offer Hearst some friendly advice on how to improve his newspapers. There is a brief glimpse too of a mean-spirited Woodrow Wilson refusing a presidential pardon for sick, old Eugene Debs, whom the patriotism police have imprisoned for speaking against American entry into the First World War. Warren G. Harding, everybody's favorite rotten president, appears a few moments later and, with a magnanimity we expect of superior presidents, sets Debs free. Richard Nixon, never famous for magnanimity, passes cruel judgment on the haberdashery of President George Bush the Elder, not neglecting to comment for good measure on Bush's character: "The guy's got no guts."

Abraham Lincoln is not here, but the widow Mary Todd Lincoln is seen in a strange shipboard encounter with Sarah Bernhardt, and Lincoln's son Robert is denounced not only for becoming a tool of greedy capitalists, but also for treating his mother badly. I am not sure whether to believe that Mary Todd actually met Sarah Bernhardt at sea but have no reason to disbelieve it, so include it here because of a weakness for amazing stories and because Marguerite Young, a human encyclopedia of bizarre American political history, writes it as gospel in her *Harp Song for a Radical*. In the same vein I accept Murray Kempton's report that John L. Lewis, one of labor's most fractious warriors, once killed a mad mule in a coal mine with his bare fists. Kempton was a reporter who almost always knew what he was talking about.

To counterbalance so many politicians there is a large company of people here who had no yearning whatever for the presidency, among them Joe DiMaggio, Marilyn Monroe, James Thurber, Harold Ross, Malcolm X, and Martin Luther King, not to mention a bearded lady, a nudist queen, and a man dedicated to stamping out profane language in New York City. Benito Mussolini and Adolf Hitler make cameo appearances, striving—and failing—to master the art of the American newspaper column. All appear courtesy of a dozen or so authors whose works caught the eye of Robert Silvers of *The New York Review of Books* between 1997 and 2001. At various times each book arrived at my door with a seductive note suggesting I might be interested in saying something about it, never asking if I would "review" it.

I disliked book reviewing, since it seemed to require passing public judgment on the work of other writers. Writing a book is hard work. It may take a year, or two, or three out of a writer's life. Disposing of it in a few hundred words, as the typical book review does, seemed to deny the author a justice commensurate with his toil. Somebody must do it of course, for no review at all is harder for a writer to endure than even a bad review. To me it seemed a work better left to others. If Robert Silvers had asked for "reviews," none of these pieces would have been written.

Instead, each book arrived, usually without warning, invariably accompanied by a brief note suggesting it might be such good reading that I just might end up wishing to write perhaps four thousand words about it. This was a beguiling invitation, for it suggested the editor would sit still for a relatively long essay. For someone who had spent thirty-seven years writing a newspaper column two and a quarter inches wide and eighteen inches long, this would be a new and challenging exercise. Since I was about to retire from *The New York Times* after half a century in daily journalism, I was looking for something new to do, preferably something entirely different.

The column I had been writing for the *Times* since 1962 permitted great freedom to fool around with various literary forms but could never exceed that eighteen-inch length. Writing effectively in that space was not quite as hard as staging a ballet in a telephone booth, but it often felt that way. It usually took only 700 to 750 words to fill the column, and years of writing constantly in this miniature form eventually conditioned my mind to think only 750-word thoughts.

Writing that column for an employer as tolerant as the *Times* was a delightful job, perhaps one of the most enviable in all journalism, but it also locked the mind in a 750-word prison. Escaping it was all very well, but was it still possible to learn something different? The books Robert Silvers was sending offered an opportunity to find out. Some of them went back barely opened. This book is composed of what I felt like writing about some of the ones I read.

Why did these books seem more interesting than those that went back unread? Age, most likely. I had begun to enjoy looking back more than one does in the summery years of life. The books that seemed most interesting were books that took me touring back into my own past.

Thus, David Nasaw's biography of Hearst: Hearst had occupied an important part of my childhood, and not all of it pleasantly. He provided my first newspaper job: as a twelve-year-old entrepreneur running a two-block home-delivery route for his *Baltimore News-Post* and *Sunday American*. Opening Nasaw's book affected me as the madeleine affected Proust. Suddenly the sinister darkness of pre-dawn Baltimore's abandoned streets rose out of memory's mists, and it was 1939, a freezing Sunday morning, and I plodded the gaslit streets depositing *The Katzenjammer Kids* and the somber reflections of Dr. Karl von Weygand, "dean of foreign correspondents," on the doorsteps of slumbering southwest Baltimore.

The three years I worked that job seemed endless, and I sometimes hated it. Hearst was squeezing each of his newsboys out of a few pennies every week by making us pay for the excess papers with which he overloaded us, but I did not know that at the time, and, being only twelve and ardent for capitalism, would only have been amused at the old boy's ingenuity if I had known it.

There were glories too. As a reward for feats of salesmanship (ten new subscribers one spring!), he once treated me to an all-day visit to Atlantic City. Another time I was rewarded with my first rubber-chicken hotel banquet, and that night I learned that the world contained salad forks and soup spoons. With his newspapers, which were irresistible reading for twelve-year-olds, he also acquainted me with the existence of "love nests" and the arresting fact that a woman of "statuesque" proportions was often to be found in one, sometimes lying defunct in "a pool of blood."

He was still a heavy American presence when I reached college, where advanced thinkers insisted that he be despised as an enemy of the oppressed classes. We were all too young to have been alive when he was being despised as a dangerous leftist, so I went along with the crowd and despised him as a rightist.

By century's end the Hearst of my youth had turned into someone who looked like Orson Welles, so thoroughly had *Citizen Kane* created the impression that it was a daringly fictionalized biography of Hearst. It does not take long immersion in Nasaw's book to see how thoroughly Orson Welles deceived us. Hearst was nothing like Welles's misogynistic, lonely, unloved Kane. Welles turned the unique inventor of the modern media empire into a cliché—the rich man whose money can't buy happiness.

Marguerite Young's strange book about Eugene Debs was irresistible because Debs was a railroad man. Three of my uncles had been railroad men—one a blacksmith, one a brakeman, one a steam locomotive engineer—and my stepfather was a locomotive fireman when he married into the family. Debs had been a fireman too. Editing the union newspaper, he kept track of the gory lists of railroad men dismembered, scalded to death, crushed, or permanently crippled on the job each month, and he was outraged by the indifference of railroad tycoons and the governments that protected them. Debs tried fighting them through political and union action, but in an age when businessmen and government leaders ran the nation for their mutual benefit he was destined to die a loser.

Marguerite Young's book turned out to be a mind-expanding tour through branches of nineteenth-century cultural history that shaped the country's political struggles. It was often astonishing and sometimes irritating. Now, two years after first reading it, I am still uncertain whether it is a rare and wonderful history of American political culture, or just a very strange book.

The books about Barry Goldwater, Richard Nixon, and the poisonous relationship between Lyndon Johnson and Robert F. Kennedy fetched me because I had spent a lot of my working life keeping an eye on all four and had a proprietary feeling toward stories about them. Politicians who reach the major leagues fascinate me as quarks fascinate a physicist. The closer you watch them the more baffling they seem.

Goldwater, Nixon, Johnson, and Robert Kennedy were even more baffling than most. Did Goldwater ever truly want to be president? What would Shakespeare have made of Lyndon Johnson—Falstaff or Lear, Richard III or Bolingbroke? Did the murder of Jack Kennedy account for Robert Kennedy's sense of entitlement to power and, if so, what did this say about him?

Has American politics ever produced a more extraordinary human mystery than Richard Nixon? Everything about him baffled me from the first time I covered him at a 1949 speaking engagement to the end of Monica Crowley's *Nixon in Winter* fifty years later. The passing decades brought the country a series of "new Nixons," each supposedly a new and improved version of the previous edition. The suggestion seemed to be that each previous Nixon had been flawed but reengineering had finally got everything working right at last.

My own theory is that he was one astonishingly consistent unchangeable Nixon from beginning to end, but that's another book. Monica Crowley's book presented Nixon as foxy old Grandpa chatting to a scholarly young admirer about the day-to-day contents of that subtle mind of his, all the time shaping the sad tale of his lost presidency to win the sympathy of youth. As always, it was fascinating to watch him at work.

The lives of all these midcentury politicians were intertwined with the life and death of Martin Luther King. He was probably the one indisputably great American of the century's second half. Fittingly, Taylor Branch's *Pillar of Fire* is the one indisputably monumental book discussed in this collection, and I wanted to write about it for the same reason I wanted to write about Richard Ben Cramer's book on Joe DiMaggio. Gods had walked the earth in my time, and I wanted to boast about being there when they did it.

Martin Luther King turns out to have been the genuine article, but Cramer persuaded me DiMaggio was not. He allows, however, that godhood was not DiMaggio's ambition to begin with. Cramer's picture of hard men manufacturing false gods for a gullible mass market is not a book for old men who think the world was still innocent when they were young.

Capital punishment, the subject of William McFeely's *Proximity to Death*, has been my favorite Gothic horror since 1938 when good Father Pat O'Brien persuaded James Cagney to go to the electric chair "yellow." The food ordered by condemned men for their last meals still fascinates me. Why do so many in Texas order cheeseburgers? In Arkansas a feeble-minded convict named Rickey Ray Rector —whose execution had been ostentatiously endorsed by Governor Bill Clinton to demonstrate his implacable hostility to crime—finished his entree, then asked the guards to hold the dessert so he could eat it when he got back from the execution chamber. I could no more resist saying something about Professor McFeely's book than I can resist staying up for a midnight TV viewing of Boris Karloff as *The Mummy*.

As for the pieces here discussing the works of Murray Kempton and Joseph Mitchell and several books about *The New Yorker* magazine, I will say only that they all disclose a shameless bias toward elitism in journalism. Other twentieth-century journalists may have been as splendid in their fashion as Kempton and Mitchell were in theirs, but there were none superior.

The New Yorker created by Harold Ross and sustained for decades by William Shawn was long one of the country's finest magazines. When it reached the age at which human beings too begin to go creaky and fail, people began saying it was not what it used to be. An editor of *Punch*, hearing the same complaint in an earlier generation, had said, "It never was." *The New Yorker*, however, having flaunted its excellence for so long, had created greater expectations than it was able to gratify. In New York it is not enough to be merely consistently good; failure to be consistently better than ever may be fatal.

Turmoil inside the magazine, as well as its approaching seventy-fifth anniversary, produced a flurry of books looking back, assigning blame, settling old scores, and churning up a great deal of entertaining if insignificant gossip. Such is to be expected when several literary people who have worked together in a successful enterprise start competing to tell their own story. Most of them sooner or later found the focus of their stories in William Shawn, the editorial maestro who had stayed on too long and been fired.

Coming back to this story recently, I thought perhaps it was less about love for Shawn than I had first thought, and more about self-love.

Chapter 1

THE SENSE OF SIN

MURRAY KEMPTON DISDAINED the word "journalist." He was a reporter, he said. To newspeople of his generation, it was an important distinction. For those who had taken a fancy to the trade, as he had, in the 1930s, "journalist" had the ridiculous sound of the local society reporter giving himself airs. A seasoned foreign correspondent whom I consulted in 1952 for advice about reporting from London cautioned that, over there, reporters actually called themselves "journalists." It seemed hilarious to both of us, but I was astonished, on arriving in Fleet Street, to discover that it was true.

Kempton, in his elliptical manner, explained his view of the matter by recalling a luncheon conversation with Westbrook Pegler. Once a much respected sportswriter, Pegler had turned columnist and, in that role, incessantly attacked Eleanor Roosevelt with such fury that many of his colleagues suspected he had become unhinged. During their lunch, Kempton recalled, Pegler said "he had been misunderstood by those who imagined that he had been driven crazy by Mrs. Roosevelt. That, he said, was not the case at all. 'It began,' Peg explained, 'when I quit sports and went cosmic. It finished when I began writing on Monday to be printed on Friday.'"

"That gospel," said Kempton, "has been so rooted in my heart ever since that I write every day for the next and walk wide of the cosmic and settle most happily for the local. . . ."

The modesty is beguiling, but there is about it the touch of the confidence man pretending to be a simple country lad with mud between his toes. Kempton's long career shows us a man with much more in mind than the simplicities of newspaper reporting. To make open confession of higher ambition was, of course, out of the question. The conventions of the newsroom demanded that anyone with complex ambitions keep quiet about them or accept the ridicule reserved for those who admitted to dreams of becoming the next Hemingway. High aspirations were permissible and even commonplace in every newsroom, but it was terribly bad form to announce them.

Born in 1917, Kempton had come of age during the Depression, when movies were celebrating the newspaper reporter as a glamorous champion of the persecuted and dispossessed. This movie reporter was outwardly a wisecracking cynic hardened by exposure to too many bad cops and rotten politicians, but, deep within, he was a man of moral principle. It being the 1930s, his sympathies ran against the rich and the powerful. He was Hildy Johnson saving a condemned innocent from the gallows in *The Front Page*, and he was Clark Gable teaching the snobby society dame Claudette Colbert how to dunk a working stiff's doughnut. He was, above all, one with the plain people, a man with the cheek to insult mayors, police chiefs, and bankers. With a press card stuck in the greasy band of his battered fedora, he might be miserably underpaid, but he was gloriously independent and licked no man's boots. This mythic hero of Kempton's youth was a reporter—just a plain reporter.

Well, Kempton was not just a plain reporter. He was a reporter of exceeding elegance. His prose had an intricacy that few newspaper editors would have tolerated. He was a master of irony and had the wit of a first-rate humorist, yet he brought moral judgment to bear on the day's most humdrum news events. He was concerned with sin. His grasp of the historical context of the day's headlines would have flabbergasted the plain reporters of my youth. All would have considered much of his reporting a flagrant violation of the reporter's license.

Here, chosen at random from a collection of his journalism, is a sentence he wrote while reporting a national political convention:

> But if for [Lord] Acton there was no worse heresy than that the office sanctifies the holder of it, there is for journalism no credo more sacred than that victory, however seedy, certifies the brilliance of the victor.[1]

This is not a sentence to be lightly skimmed, as reporters' sentences are supposed to be. It is an intricately filigreed eighteenth-century construction completely alien to modern American newswriting. It will be utterly baffling to most newspaper readers unwilling to pause in the day's hurlyburly, reread it two or three times, find out who Lord Acton was, then struggle with the puzzling parallel between Acton's view of heresy and journalism's sacred credo.

It is the creation of a writer, not a plain reporter. It is the work of a man learned in history, acrobatic in grammar, skilled in irony and willing to use it—as with that jeer at journalism's sacred credo—to laugh at the pretensions of his own trade. A plain reporter? Hardly. Then what? Perhaps a historian writing the story of his own time.

Kempton was a loving student of history, especially history written on the classic English model. His style is sometimes reminiscent of Gibbon, sometimes of Macaulay. Kempton himself said he most admired the Earl of Clarendon, whose seventeenth-century *History of the Rebellion* predated Gibbon by a full century.

Clarendon seems a curious passion in a man obliged to please readers of the breezier dailies, but please them Kempton did, and American reporters, most of whom would never have dared try it

---

1. *Rebellions, Perversities, and Main Events* (Times Books, 1994), p. 526.

themselves, revered him for pulling it off. He was evidence that, though theirs might be a raffish trade, there was more to it than those tired old corpses lying in pools of blood and eternally posturing presidents droning away in ghostwritten prose.

In the mid-1950s Kempton published *Part of Our Time*, his one full-length book about the history of the era of his youth, which has been out of print since the Sixties. It is now reissued in the Modern Library series, which confers "classic" status, I suppose.[2] Classic or not, it is good to have it back in print, for it is a valuable and entertaining text on the destruction of the radical left in American politics. In a society where many now recoil from the word "liberal," how many even know that not so long ago there was a real American left? And that the word "radical" did not refer to Republican Christers out to turn government into an agent of Puritanism but to people dreaming of a society economically perfected, if necessary, through violence?

Kempton, himself a man of the left, cannot resist an ironic smile at the way the dream ended.

> The social revolutionary of the thirties thought that he was prepared to die by violence. He thought that he was prepared for an America destroyed by war and fascism. His imagination covered, in fact, almost every disaster except the one which has now overtaken him.
>
> For he could not have known that, within twenty years, he would live in an America made glorious according to every dream of the economic materialist. Its wealth, its resources, its almost universally exalted living standards would not have seemed to him possible except in the triumph of his own revolutionary program.

The leftists of his study had been young and vital in the Thirties

---

2. *Part of Our Time: Some Ruins and Monuments of the Thirties* (Modern Library, 1998).

but, at the time Kempton wrote, most were relics of interest only to Red-hunting congressmen. His subtitle calls them "Some Ruins and Monuments of the Thirties," but ruins far outnumber monuments in his cast. Walter Reuther and maybe John L. Lewis and Paul Robeson are names that still have weight among people interested in American history. Even among these few, however, only geezers are likely to remember J. B. Matthews, who abandoned revolution to track Communists for the House Un-American Activities Committee, or Elizabeth Bentley, the "Red Spy Queen" of a thousand headlines.

Alger Hiss and Whittaker Chambers are here, of course. Almost everyone still remembers them. Though both were already ruins when Kempton wrote, the world always prefers a good story to a political manifesto; theirs was a good story indeed and will probably preserve them in memory for ages to come, the most subtle treatment of them remaining Kempton's.

Communism dominated the radical movement of the Thirties, and most of Kempton's subjects were Communists at one time or another. Some, like Elizabeth Bentley, turned against it and became famous for anticommunism in the Fifties. Some, like Julius Rosenberg, stayed with it and became Soviet agents.

As a student at Johns Hopkins Kempton himself belonged briefly to the Young Communist League. Joining was required, he said, to get work during his short career as a seaman. When he left the sea, he took to socialism. *Part of Our Time* has a pronounced anti-Communist flavor, at least when it comes to the Party itself. Kempton seems to believe that some of the Communists were chiefly to blame for the destruction of the traditional and honorable American radical movement. He is gentle toward the Thirties radicals who left the Party and he can be hard on some who stayed.

He returns time and again to the evil effect of communism. Clearly, Kempton was profoundly and authentically Christian, and communism's contempt for New Testament values appalled him.

Throughout his book we encounter reflections on sin, mercy, pity, and the loss of innocence. He talks of the "secular hell" awaiting those "born without innocence." He had no patience for those who were indifferent to such matters. The Communist view of them went beyond indifference into open contempt.

Thus:

> ...The Communists offer one precious, fatal boon: they take away the sense of sin. It may or may not be debatable whether a man can live without God; but, if it were possible, we should pass a law forbidding a man to live without the sense of sin.

And:

> I cannot conceal the sense that those of my subjects who became Communists were terribly flawed by their acceptance of a gospel which had no room in it for doubt or pity or mercy, and that, clutching its standard, it was inevitable that so many would set out to be redeemers and end up either policemen or the targets of policemen.

Lee Pressman is the dark figure of Kempton's story. He had arrived in Washington in the early Thirties as a legal do-gooder, but soon revealed a ruthlessness that made him valuable to men like John L. Lewis. He met Lewis when the CIO was being forged and eventually became its general counsel. Curiously, though Kempton obviously dislikes Pressman for his indifference to Christian morality, he sketches the equally ruthless Lewis as a Homeric figure too grand to be judged by normal moral standards.

> Pressman had never met a man like Lewis; there is only one. They understood each other because they understood that the

price of power and victory is a man's innocence. John Lewis had once killed a mad mule in a mine with his bare fist; and, since in those days a mule's life was worth more than a miner's, he had saved his job by covering his victim's wound with mud and telling the superintendent that it died of heart failure. He was the two prime Homeric heroes in one mold, at once Achilles and Ulysses; he went as far as strength would take him and thereafter proceeded by guile. He respected force and cunning alike; and he expected devotion.

Kempton's obvious admiration for Lewis is not diminished by the fact that he "lived somewhere beyond innocence" and "simply fought without conscience." But then, Lewis's moral deficiencies do not arise from loyalty to communism. Lee Pressman's do.

By accepting Lenin as his model, Pressman had violated the tradition of American radicalism. How so? Because Leninism was "an image of Christ inverted": whereas Christ taught that we should love our enemies, Lenin taught that we should hate our friends "if they were detected in the sin of being wrong."

Though Pressman said he had left the Party in 1935, Kempton contends he remained devoted to the Soviet Union "as the repository of the gospel in its highest form. History was enthroned there." Pressman was governed by a "religious fantasy" of communism. To a close colleague who had spoken critically of the 1937 Moscow show trials, in which Stalin was having the old Bolsheviks "tried" and shot, Pressman's reply was curt: "Do you mean, J.B., that you reject the Terror?" After that, writes Kempton, "things were never the same between them."

The terror and Stalin's show trials had dealt a shocking blow to Americans who had once given their hearts to communism. They did not make Pressman, however, recoil from the gospel, and Kempton is unforgiving. His attitude may owe something to Arthur Koestler's

Darkness at Noon. Kempton would almost certainly have read it, for it was widely read and debated in the Forties by those with an intellectual interest in the Soviet Union. In a story based on the Moscow trials, Koestler created a nightmare vision of the Stalinist state, and its effect on the American left was profound.

The novel depicts the clash between the new Communist man, Gletkin, and Rubashov, a composite of the old Bolsheviks whom Stalin had liquidated with the 1937 trials. Reviewing it in 1941, Harold Strauss noted that these legalistic travesties, like the confrontation between Gletkin and Rubashov, were "a clash between pragmatic absolutism and humanitarian democracy."

For Kempton, a champion of humanitarian democracy, Pressman was, like Gletkin, too much the pragmatic absolutist: "He seemed like a naked sword. He did not make his way by charm and sympathy but because he was an instrument more serviceable than any other in the locker. His language was the language of operations; he burned not nor blazed about the goal; he offered only to tell you how to get there."

His disapproval of Pressman should not be taken as evidence that Kempton was writing a conventional anti-Communist screed of the 1950s. Toward most of his aging radicals he was evenhanded and, toward some, affectionate. His chapter on radical novelists and playwrights of the Thirties is an amused reflection on the absurdity of trying to turn political theory into fiction. His chapter on Joseph Curran, who fought his way to the top of the National Maritime Union, could have been written by a loving son.

The Hollywood Ten leave him marveling at the disparity between the fame heaped on them by congressional investigators and the triviality of their leftist accomplishments. He presents a representative list of movies written by apparent Communists in the Thirties. It includes *Little Orphan Annie*, *The Saint in New York*, and *Algiers*, a romance in which Charles Boyer, playing Pepe le Moko, asked Hedy Lamarr to "come with me to the Casbah." Kempton finds them vain, ineffectual, and slightly contemptible: "Life was a scenario to most of them: the Comintern was a musical and Spain the Rose Bowl."

He gives us Paul Robeson as a noble but sad and lonely giant, isolated from America's less talented, less lucky, less well-schooled black masses. To them, the white man's radical politics had no apparent relevance to the black condition in America. Kempton is sympathetic to the suffering Robeson underwent for his leftist political views, but his black hero is A. Philip Randolph, who taught Pullman porters that black people had to take their destiny in their own hands.

Kempton's chapter on Hiss and Chambers flows from his belief that Hiss was indeed a Communist as Chambers said. It is the why of Hiss's communism that interests him, and his own past prompts him to a curious theory. Like Hiss, Kempton had grown up in the Bolton Hill section of Baltimore, the city's "heartland of shabby gentility." Both had gone to Johns Hopkins University. Reflecting on how that dull, bourgeois world had affected his own life, Kempton wonders about Hiss: Could it have been a sense of guilt that made Hiss a disciplined Communist?

> Men like Alger Hiss do not have to become Communists, at least in the West; it is an act of will. Membership in the Party is an inconvenience; its duties are much more material than its rewards. There are a variety of reasons that could impel a man toward this unattractive discipline. One of them may be the sense of guilt—the guilt of inaction in a time of action, the guilt of serving oneself first in the face of the knowledge that it is better to serve others, the guilt of unexpressed aspirations which are different from the aspirations of your own kind.
>
> The men who become Communists out of that sense of guilt are spoiled priests.
>
> ... The terrible conflict between [Hiss's] private self and his public conduct is the most compelling reason why he could have joined the Communist Party.

The left discussed in *Part of Our Time* was destroyed in the 1950s. It had been born of economic suffering in the Depression and seemed irrelevant during the postwar boom. There was something slightly musty about its bellicose rhetoric, left over from the bellicose Thirties. It all seemed rather long ago and far away. Who remembered Hoovervilles? The Okies were about to turn Orange County into a fortress of Republican conservatism. A new generation didn't know that Spain had once been important or that Joe Hill had been killed by the copper bosses or that Douglas MacArthur had routed the Bonus Army out of Washington. They had forgotten the sit-down strikes, the Homestead riot, Henry Ford's goons, dish night at the movies, and the electrocution of Sacco and Vanzetti.

It is a terrible thing in America to be out-of-date, but the radical left had an even heavier burden to shoulder. There was something suspiciously foreign about it. Karl Marx, communism, faraway Russia, all that about uniting the world's workers, overthrowing reactionary capitalism—it was definitely suspiciously foreign.

The dominance that communism had gained in the Thirties became lethal to the movement once Stalin's terror spread into Europe. Soviet acquisition of the atomic bomb and Soviet seizure of the Central European states created a suspicion in America that communism was a very nasty enemy. The American left, with its old Communist influences, was about to be crushed. The flood of former Communists talking about Red spies concealed in high places and eating away at democracy's innards made for sensational headlines. Now it took courage to admit that one had once been a warrior of the left. The summer of 1950 brought war in Korea—against communism. And of course there was, for the left, news that American communism had helped provide Stalin with the atomic bomb.

The unsurprising results included Richard Nixon and Joseph McCarthy, loyalty oaths, suppression of the right to travel, and jailings of persons too principled to "name names" of people they knew to be Communists. Those who were "named" could expect to be fired from whatever job they might hold. For the American left, it was a slaughter. Kempton's history was being written as the last remnants of the movement were being mopped up by congressional committees.

To speak of "the left" in American politics today betrays either indifference to political reality or a taste for demagoguery. There has been no left of intellectual consequence since Kempton wrote. The Vietnam era produced a transient movement called "the New Left," but it had no discernible intellectual roots. It was born in a spontaneous combustion of hatred for the Vietnam War, but, with such slogans as "make love, not war," it was scarcely a threat to the capitalist system.

It is hard to determine what conservative pamphleteers have in mind when they whack away at "the left" and "leftists." They are like ghost hunters searching an abandoned house. More careful conservatives use the words sparingly and concentrate on expunging "liberalism." Today's meaningless political language asks us to think of "liberalism" as a malevolent doctrine which, if not stamped out, could replace communism as chief threat to the republic.

Such malarkey has replaced ideological debate in American politics, with the result that recent presidential campaigns have seemed brain dead. The Reagan campaign of 1984 pleaded with the electorate to re-elect the Gipper because it was morning in America. In 1992 George Bush spoke of "the vision thing" in a way that made it clear he didn't have one. He also made it clear that anybody who could be identified by "the L-word"—yes, sinister old "liberalism"—ought to be shunned.

The spreading inanity found President Clinton in 1996 coming out firmly against smoking by children. He was elected as a New Democrat. Yes, Virginia, there is a New Democrat. A New Democrat is a Democrat who stands slightly to the right of President Eisenhower. By New Democrat standards, Nelson Rockefeller would have been—do we dare use the L-word?

Chapter 2

A BOY'S LIFE

FROM MARK TWAIN and Theodore Roosevelt to Steven Spielberg and Bill Clinton the evidence is overwhelming: the adult American male's dream of paradise is eternal boyhood. David Nasaw's Hearst is a sublime example.[1] Nasaw presents him at age ten in London asking his mother to buy him the royal family's carriage horses and in his seventies throwing costume parties for movie stars—Gary Cooper coming as Dr. Fu Manchu, Groucho Marx as Rex the Wonder Horse, Hearst presiding as cowboy gunslinger, Tyrolean peasant, circus ringmaster. In the years between ten and seventy-five he builds himself a castle on 60,000 acres and furnishes it with a private zoo, tries to start some wars, cruises Europe like a king on a royal progress chatting up the mighty and buying any and all treasures that catch his fancy. He hires Winston Churchill, puts both Mussolini and Hitler on his payroll, runs for president.

Not since *Tahara, Boy King of the Yucatan* has a book so delighted my inner boy. There is much more. How about a good war story? In this one, war has been declared against the Spanish in Cuba, and Will wants to be there, see the action, scoop his newspaper rivals with on-the-scene stuff. (Only his mother and very close pals call him Will, of

---

1. *The Chief: The Life of William Randolph Hearst* (Houghton Mifflin, 2000).

course, but, aesthetically, it's the only possible name in this episode.) His rival Teddy (Roosevelt, that is) has already beaten him to Cuba, bringing along his very own personal cavalry—cowboys, naturally— and is looking for a hill to charge.

Lacking cavalry, Will rents a steamship, loads it with printing presses, ice, medical supplies, cooks, stewards, and "food fit for a king." Also correspondents, illustrators, editors, telegraphers, and two showgirls he's been escorting around New York for the past year or so. Ashore, he and his warrior journalists blunder into enemy gunfire which wounds one of his correspondents. "I'm sorry you're hurt," Will tells his bleeding colleague, "but wasn't it a splendid fight? We must beat every paper in the world." And leaving his fallen pal to medics on the beach, off he sails for Jamaica to file an exclusive eyewitness story. What fun!

Joy, alas, is ever but an instant away from despair in the boyish heart, and the war is scarcely ended before Will realizes that Teddy has whipped him in the struggle for glory. "I made the mistake of my life in not raising the cowboy regiment I had in mind before Roosevelt raised his," Will writes his mother. "I really believe I brought on the war but I failed to score in the war."

Cuba has made Teddy a national hero; he has been drafted to run for governor of New York. That happens to be a job Will wants, as well as the presidency of the United States. "I had my chance and failed to grab it," he tells his mother, "and I suppose I must sit on the fence now and watch the procession go by.... I'm a failure.... Outside of the grief it would give you I had better be in a Santiago trench than where I am.... Goodnight, Mama dear. Take care of yourself. Don't let me lose you. I wish you were here tonight. I feel about eight years old—and very blue."

Did Hearst truly believe, as he writes here, that he had "brought on" the Spanish-American War of 1898? The popular notion was that he had, but Nasaw thinks this absurd. The United States would have declared war "even had William Randolph Hearst never gone into publishing," he argues. Americans were itching for an empire, and decrepit Spain's was ripe for the plucking. If Americans really believed Hearst had given them this chance to strut in battle, while picking up the Philippines as a bonus, it merely proved he was a "genius as a self-promoter," says Nasaw. He also doubts that Hearst ever issued the famous command to Frederick Remington: "You furnish the pictures, and I'll furnish the war." The only record he finds of such an exchange appears in the autobiography of a Hearst colleague written in 1901. Hearst himself, in a letter to the *Times* of London in 1907, said the notion that he was responsible for the war was "clotted nonsense."

Still he had tried hard enough to start a war. War would be a good story, good for business, a chance for a young man with get-up-and-go to do great things, make a reputation for himself. And have some fun too. The situation in Cuba had all the elements Hearst's New York *Journal* loved. "Here," writes Nasaw, "was raw material for tales of corruption more horrific than any yet told. The villains were lecherous and bloodthirsty Spanish officials and army officers; the victims, innocent Cuban women and children; the heroes, crusading *Journal* reporters and their publisher." The very proper Spanish General Valeriano Weyler became "Butcher" Weyler, who, if the *Journal*'s "credible witnesses" could be believed, killed all his prisoners on the spot, not sparing helpless hospital patients. These, said an editorial, were "the methods of the Turkish savages in Armenia." Only "a righteous crusade" could drive them out of the hemisphere.

And so on. Almost all of it was baloney, but what a lovely story it made, so long as nobody sent a real reporter, a mistake Hearst made in 1897 by hiring Richard Harding Davis. Davis never found an army in the field, heard a shot fired, or saw a guerrilla warrior. He was disgusted. "All Hearst wants is my name and I will give him that only if it will be signed to a different sort of a story from those they have been printing," he wrote home. He never did find any fighting.

It won't do to explain Hearst solely as an exuberant juvenile. That would make for a coherent explanation, and for Hearst there is no coherent explanation. He cast a giant shadow, but his life had no theme. For a biographer he is like a six-ring circus: all spectacle and no plot. Watch the lion tamer and you miss the clowns; look up and see acrobats fly through space, look down and see women dancing on the backs of galloping horses. Thus with Hearst. It is not a life, it is an extravaganza.

Now he is a newspaper publisher, now a movie producer, now a lover of women, now a left-wing radical, now a right-wing reactionary, stage-door Johnny, Red hunter, compulsive buyer of things, things, things. Though going into bankruptcy, he splurges the modern equivalent of $5 million on antiques, art, and real estate. "I'm afraid I'm like a dipsomaniac with a bottle," he tells a colleague. "They keep sending me these catalogs and I can't resist them."

Nasaw had access to a storehouse (literally) of previously unpublished documents, and there is a great deal here that was not available when W. A. Swanberg wrote his *Citizen Hearst* forty years ago. This includes correspondence with his parents and with twentieth-century world leaders, many of whom wrote for Hearst's papers. This material —tons of it by Nasaw's estimate—has been stored for decades in a Bronx warehouse and a Hearst Corporation building at San Simeon. A lot in the new documents will be valuable to scholars, and wire traffic between Hearst and his editors will be especially interesting to journalists.

Here, for example, is a priceless piece of comedy in which Hitler and Mussolini show how to get under Hearst's skin. Both wrote for him in the early 1930s, and each was an editor's nightmare. Hearst's editorial manager, Vanneman Ranck, was at the point of contact with the pair, and his wire messages to Hearst reveal a man near the boiling point. He reports constant trouble with Mussolini: "ponderous" prose, dull subject matter, copy constantly late.

Then—what's this! Mussolini's latest piece disagrees with Hearst's view on the European war debt. Hearst is furious. This gives Ranck a chance to argue for dropping Il Duce from the payroll. Unless reined in, he cautions, Mussolini will try to "make us take any old pot-boiling topic that he pleases at any time at twelve hundred dollars per article. Not only has Mussolini been endeavoring to work off some very uninteresting subjects but in spite of all our admonitions has been providing some of them so late as to miss our [deadlines]." Hearst agrees that it's time to crack down: "Have noted that Mussolini has been less interesting of late.... There is no reason why we should take and pay for dull stuff." But Mussolini hangs on.

When Hitler goes on the payroll he is still a minor player in German politics and is worth only a small fee. As he turns into Der Führer he demands better pay. Then we enter Chaplin territory with Ranck wiring Hearst that Hitler won't write a piece Hearst wants "unless we willing pay him as much as pay Mussolini. Frankly do not believe he is worth as much as Mussolini. Do you? What would you think of Goering?" Soon Hermann Goering has replaced Hitler as Hearst's inside expert in Germany and turns out to be a shameless chiseler, forever trying to squeeze "the Chief" for more money.

It is Hearst as newspaperman who matters today. He pioneered in the intermingling of news and entertainment for the mass market, which is to say, modern media. Nasaw says he was also the first "to understand that the communications media were potentially more powerful than the parties and their politicians." Perhaps, but if he really understood it, why did he try so hard to promote himself into political office? Would Rupert Murdoch want to fritter away his time being president of the United States?

At the height of his power Hearst owned twenty-six daily newspapers in eighteen cities. Between the gaslight age and World War II he was the colossus of American journalism. Unlike the boardroom finaglers who run our modern "media" conglomerates, he was a highly skilled news-paperman who could edit a paper, cover a story, and write an eloquent editorial. He had learned all this by doing. At Harvard he showed no interest in learning anything, but after being expelled he threw himself into intense study of Joseph Pulitzer's New York *World*, and went home to San Francisco at the age of twenty-three to apply Pulitzer's ideas to the moribund *Examiner*. The *Examiner* was a gift from his father, who cared nothing for journalism and apparently thought young Will wasn't up to much more than running a failing newspaper. He had a genius for selling newspapers. He swiftly turned around the *Examiner* and headed east to take charge of the New York *Journal* and go head-to-head against Pulitzer's *World* for the yellow-journalism championship.

Hearst believed talent was more vital to success than the quarterly earnings report and paid big money to fill his papers with it. Enthralled by the high quality of Joseph Pulitzer's staff, he simply offered the best of them huge salaries and hired them for himself. He was innovative and inventive. His first columnist was Ambrose Bierce. He invented the "sob sister." He gave America the Katzenjammer Kids, Maggie and Jiggs, and Flash Gordon in beautifully printed color. He established his own news wire service and created new magazines. With the advent of the movie camera, he flooded theaters with newsreels. He kept daily watch on his papers across the country, sending instructions on how to play the news, phoning editors in the night with new orders, keeping everyone forever reminded that "the Chief" was in charge and "the Chief" never slept.

Being the colossus of journalism was not enough, though; he wanted to be president. This is puzzling, for he was temperamentally unfit for elective politics and disliked politicians, who in turn disliked and, more importantly, distrusted him.

He was hankering for the White House when he and Teddy, who also had the itch, competed for glory in Cuba. The two were born to be enemies, and their mutual hatred was the stuff of trashy fiction. Each had been popular at Harvard, but in different ways. Hearst's popularity owed a lot to the lavish way he spent money to entertain. The good Harvard clubs accepted him, but this did not qualify him for admission to fancy Boston society where Teddy was at ease. Teddy was old money; Hearst was new money of the rawest kind.

Was he sensitive to being slightly déclassé? Since Nasaw is not a psychoanalyzer we are free to guess for ourselves. Most of Hearst's classmates would have come from what society editors used to call "good" families, meaning that the source of their wealth had been long forgotten. Harvard in those days was the home office of "good" families. The Hearsts were not a "good" family, and by Harvard standards the source of their money was not a pretty sight.

George Hearst was a Missouri farmer who went to California in the gold rush and ended up with big stakes in Anaconda, the Ophir Mine, and the Comstock Lode. These made him rich enough to buy a seat in the United States Senate. Nasaw describes a formidable figure: "uncouth, loud, and semiliterate, seldom changed his shirtfront, wore his beard long, bushy, and ragged at the edges, spit tobacco juice, liked nothing better for dinner than what he called hog and hominy, and had not seen the inside of a church in decades."

After hitting it big, George had gone back to Missouri, married Phoebe Apperson, a former schoolteacher half his age, and begat a son. For the next twenty years he made himself scarce after setting up wife and child in elegant style on a San Francisco hilltop. George loved them but loved mining more, and mining was a business that kept a man far from home most of the time. Or so he explained.

Phoebe dominated the boy's life. She was not going to raise a hog-and-hominy man. She would polish him, educate him, make him a gentleman, and see him married to a suitable wife. While spoiling him she was also tyrannizing him, conditioning him to fear her in a subdued respectable way. She had what it took to make him see things her way even into his middle age, for her husband's will had left the entire Hearst estate to her, nothing to young Will. Hearst was fifty-six years old before Phoebe's death finally made him financially independent. By then she had used the money weapon to end his engagement to an aspiring actress and to drive away the mistress he had kept for ten years and loved deeply.

Phoebe could make him go to Harvard, but she couldn't make him study. Books bored him. (If in his entire lifetime Hearst read a single book that influenced his thinking, Nasaw doesn't mention it.) He liked to throw parties and enjoyed the usual campus hell-raising. After three years of good times and rotten grades Harvard asked him to leave and not come back.

What Phoebe produced was a big shy mama's boy capable of deep and lasting love for women but uneasy with men. From men he wanted loyalty, deference, respect, obedience. He wanted colleagues to call him "the Chief." They did and he made some of them very rich. When it came to men, he didn't make friends, he acquired retinues. This was not a natural candidate for the presidency.

The gregarious Teddy was. "It is impossible to measure the depths of his loathing for Roosevelt," says Nasaw. He thought Teddy "a charlatan" and "preening aristocrat." Just before Teddy's Cuba adventures, Hearst's New York *Journal* had attacked him for wearing elegant haberdashery—pink shirts and a tasseled silk sash instead of a vest. When the hero of San Juan Hill was made the Republican candidate for governor of New York, Hearst's cartoonists and writers produced constant ridicule and abuse. "The Theodore Roosevelt that was, was a humbug," said a typical editorial. "The Theodore Roosevelt that is, is a prideless office-seeker."

Teddy, who always seemed to come out on top, won anyhow and eventually went on to be president. From the White House he avenged himself with gusto. Hearst, he told an English editor, not for attribution of course, was "the most potent single influence for evil" in American life. Then, when Hearst himself ran for governor of New York, Teddy did him in.

Basically, he accused Hearst of being complicit in the 1901 assassination of President McKinley. Before the assassination Hearst had attacked McKinley with such savage abuse that some people said he had inspired the assassin to kill. Now in 1906 with Hearst running for governor of New York, Roosevelt struck. Being president, Roosevelt could hardly do such a nasty piece of work himself, so he wrapped Secretary of State Elihu Root in presidential authority and sent him to address a New York political rally.

"I say to you, with the President's authority," Root began, "that he regards Mr. Hearst to be wholly unfit to be Governor." Then, after touching up Hearst as "an insincere, self-seeking demagogue," Root became serious:

> In President Roosevelt's first message to Congress, in speaking of the assassin of McKinley, he spoke of him as inflamed "by the reckless utterances of those who, on the stump and in the public press, appeal to the dark and evil spirits of malice and greed, envy and sullen hatred." ... I say, by the President's authority, that in penning these words, with the horror of President McKinley's murder fresh before him, he had Mr. Hearst specifically in mind. And I say, by the President's authority, that what he thought of Mr. Hearst then he thinks of Mr. Hearst now.

Teddy's blow came just four days before the election, leaving Hearst no time to recover. He lost the governorship by 60,000 votes out of a total 1.5 million cast.

Roosevelt was only one of many who yearned to put the boot into Hearst. He had a gift for making enemies. Al Smith despised him so thoroughly that in 1922 he virtually read him out of the Democratic Party. In 1904 when Hearst campaigned as a Bryan Populist, *The New York Times*, a voice of hard-money Democrats, called him a rabble-rouser standing "for absolutely nothing but the arraying of class against class."

New York's *Evening Post*, normally the voice of calm decorum, declared that if Hearst ran for president, "gutters would be dragged" and "sewers laid open," then went fortissimo:

> *An agitator we can endure; an honest radical we can respect; a fanatic we can tolerate; but a low voluptuary trying to sting his jaded senses to a fresh thrill by turning from private to public corruption is a new horror in American politics.*

Even people who supported him politically were uneasy about him. Lincoln Steffens, seeking to understand why, interviewed Hearst when he ran for governor. Here was America's "number one radical" running for an office but "one step away from the White House," yet he was a mystery. Why "plutocrats" detested him was obvious, wrote Steffens. If Hearst did what he said he would do, "it means that this child of the privileged class will really try to abolish privilege in the United States!"

But why was he disliked even by those who agreed with his progressive policies? Steffens concluded that it was because he was an aspiring dictator. Hearst, he wrote, used money "as a substitute for persuasion, charm, humor, pleadings.... He does not work with; he does not support...the other leaders of reform. He does not know who they are. Mr. Hearst is not a part of the general reform movement; he simply has a movement of his own. This isn't democratic, that is plutocratic; autocratic. Mr. Hearst is a boss."

Did Hearst really have any firmly held political ideas beyond the notion that the country needed a man it could call "the Chief"? In youth he adopted Bryan's populism. This made him a radical in the sound-money culture of the eastern business world, but it also did wonders for newspaper circulation among the struggling left-of-center urban masses with no love for bankers. As the years passed he followed the well-beaten path from reformer to fogey commonly taken by Americans as age wrings the juice out of them. Hearst, the forty-year-old rabble-rouser, agitator, radical, and fanatic—not to mention voluptuary—spent his seventies raging at FDR, cursing taxes, and hounding Reds.

The great enemy of his old age— how history loves its little jokes— was another Roosevelt. Like Hearst, FDR was also a rich, spoiled mother's boy, also a Democrat as reform-minded as Hearst had been in the old days. If Hearst had had any political instinct he would have realized that 1935 was no year to go to battle with Roosevelt. In the end his fury at FDR hastened his empire into bankruptcy.

What sent him around the bend was a soak-the-rich tax plan being prepared by Roosevelt. As one of the inevitable soakees, Hearst, already a dedicated Red-hunter, attacked FDR as the American Marx. The tax plan, he advised his main editorial writer, was "a bastard product of Communism and demagogic democracy, a mongrel creation which might accurately be called demo-communism, evolved by a composite personality which might be labeled Stalin Delano Roosevelt."

This inevitably alienated his papers' traditional working-class readership, which loved FDR. The Depression was already shrinking Hearst's newspaper revenues. Now Roosevelt supporters on the left organized a dangerously effective boycott. Nasaw is especially good on details of the bankruptcy and the unavailing efforts of Hearst's old friend Joseph P. Kennedy to persuade him to cut costs, pare his holdings, and restructure his companies. Kennedy was still well connected at the White House at this time, and soon even FDR was sending business advice through a Hearst colleague: "I advise him to get rid of his poorest papers, to print more news, not to print so many features, keep just the good ones, and to kill his editorial page." It was too late; the till was empty; the banks took charge. Although Hearst was allowed to keep editorial control of his papers, his salary was cut, dividend payments on his preferred stock were canceled, and—the ultimate degradation—he was ordered to pay rent and costs of upkeep if he stayed at San Simeon.

Besides contributing to the business catastrophe, the boycott by the end of the 1930s had made Hearst's name synonymous with right-wing reaction, and, for some, fascism. Nasaw obviously thinks Hearst has been painted too deep-dyed a villain over the past sixty years. He had his nasty moments, Nasaw seems to be saying, and they are not to be overlooked, but he also had his splendid moments. He made important contributions to progressive reform before he choked on the New Deal. On his contributions to journalism Nasaw quotes H.L. Mencken, writing in 1927 when Hearst had started drifting rightward:

> [Hearst] shook up old bones, and gave the blush of life to pale cheeks. The American newspapers, for a generation before [his] advent, had been going down hill steadily.... The American mob was rapidly becoming literate, but they were making no rational effort to reach it. Here Hearst showed the way.... He did not try to lift up the mob, like Pulitzer; he boldly leaped down to its level. Was the ensuing uproar all evil? I doubt it. Hearst not only vastly augmented the enterprise of the whole American press; he also forced it into some understanding of the rights and aspirations of the common man.

Nasaw credits him with an important political contribution. In Hearst's fight against FDR, he writes, "he set the terms for the counter-progressive ideological assault that would enter—and, at times, dominate—the nation's political discourse from the mid-1930s onward."

Hearst was an impudent boy wonder of twenty-three when he took over the San Francisco *Examiner* in the 1880s and started tormenting Joseph Pulitzer. Orson Welles, another impudent boy wonder, was twenty-five when he resolved in 1940 to have some sport with Hearst. By then Hearst was in his seventies, an age not readily charmed by the antic impudence of boy wonderhood. He was unamused by *Citizen Kane*, a movie with which Welles and his screenwriter Herman Mankiewicz obviously expected to torment him. Did Hearst personally order the famous campaign to suppress *Kane*? Nasaw finds no fingerprints, but the zeal with which Hearst's employees and powerful Hollywood colleagues worked to kill it might make even Inspector Clouseau suspicious.

Hearst could hardly have been flattered by seeing himself turned into "Charles Foster Kane," but the movie's representation of the women in his life must have seemed vile and insupportable. For all his faults, Hearst was a devoted lover of women, and he deeply respected those he loved. In the movie's "maliciously false portraits" of them, writes Nasaw,

> Kane's mother is pathologically cold and unloving; his wife is an anti-Semite and social snob; his mistress is mindless, untalented, a drunk who becomes a shrill harpie, possessed of one of the screen's most gratingly annoying voices.

The portrait of Hearst himself is relatively warm, made so by the natural buoyancy and *joie de vivre* of Welles himself, who played the role. Pauline Kael's essay on the film sees Charles Foster Kane as a well-worn Hollywood cliché, the spiritually empty rich man whose millions "can buy everything except what counts—love." Thus the great man's mistress—in real life she was Marion Davies—is cartooned as "a silly, ordinary nothing of a girl, as if everything in his life were synthetic, his passion vacuous, and the object of it a cipher."

Nasaw's Hearst has little in common with Welles's Kane:

> Both were powerful; both were enormously wealthy; both had big houses and big egos. But Welles's Kane is a cartoon-like caricature of a man who is hollowed out on the inside, forlorn,

defeated, solitary because he cannot command the total obedience, loyalty, devotion, and love of those around him. Hearst, to the contrary, never regarded himself as a failure, never recognized defeat, never stopped loving Marion [Davies] or his wife. He did not, at the end of his life, run away from the world to entomb himself in a vast, gloomy art-choked hermitage.

Citizen Kane was a box-office failure in 1941, but not necessarily because of the campaign to suppress it. Nasaw observes quite correctly that it was simply not a movie to fetch the mass audience in 1941. It was dark and experimental; there was no boy-meets-and-gets-girl, no chase, no triumph by virtue, no happy ending.

Hearst's love life was far more interesting than Kane's. His first mistress has no counterpart in *Citizen Kane*. She was Tessie Powers, a waitress from Cambridge. They met while he was at Harvard, and their relationship lasted more than ten years. When he went west to take over the *Examiner* he took Tessie with him, and they lived together in Sausalito. She went with him to Europe. A ten-year relationship suggests genuine devotion, but Phoebe did not intend to have a waitress for her daughter-in-law. Because no amount of frowning seemed to convey the message to her son, she finally exercised the power of the purse. She confronted Tessie and perhaps, though Nasaw thinks it unlikely, even threatened her with jail unless she left California. More likely, he suggests, she bought Tessie out with a pleasant sum of money. Hearst was crushed.

When he went back east to take over the New York *Journal* he lived a raffish nocturnal life and became a well-known stage-door Johnny along Broadway. In the late 1890s, he met Millicent Willson, a sixteen-year-old chorus girl from Brooklyn, married her when she was twenty-one, and had five sons by her. They remained married until his death, although Marion Davies became the great love of the last half of his life.

Phoebe Hearst hated his marriage. A chorus girl! He was now forty years old, however, a bit long in the tooth for bullying by Mother, and he had just been elected to Congress—the only elective office he ever held. Sound politics required him to marry Millicent or leave her. Nasaw thinks she was "the perfect companion for him. She was a stunning-looking woman, rather tall, with unblemished pale skin, dark hair, and piercingly dark eyes. She was also devoted to Hearst and having been with him for five years now, knew him as well as anyone else."

Marion Davies appeared in 1915. Millicent was thirty-five, Hearst was fifty-two, and Marion was eighteen, another showgirl. He first saw her in a new Irving Berlin musical. It is unclear how long the affair had run before Millicent finally intervened in 1925. Millicent was now a formidable woman, mother of five sons, and a figure in New York society. She and Hearst agreed that divorce would be ruinous for him, bad for their sons, and financially unsound for her. They stayed married and on good terms, and Millicent continued to live on a grand scale.

Marion Davies soon became the subject of gossip throughout the land. Hearst bankrolled efforts to make her a Hollywood star. Movie people agreed she had talent, especially for comedy, but Hearst couldn't bear to let her look foolish on the screen. This spoiled any chance of her becoming a "screwball comedy" star of the 1930s like Carole Lombard. When he faced bankruptcy she gave him her money, jewels, and real estate, to help him keep his newspapers.

The two were to be lovers for thirty-six years, never to marry, living their final years together, he tottering and frail, she struggling with alcohol, but the two of them still in love as only long-married old people can be. When he died Millicent came for the funeral, and Marion stayed away.

In her essay on *Citizen Kane*, Pauline Kael observes that what really happened in Hearst's love life was a better story than Welles and Mankiewicz put on film: Hearst "took a beautiful, warm-hearted girl and made her the best-known kept woman in America and the butt of an infinity of dirty jokes, and he did it out of love and the blindness of love."

Chapter 3

ONLY IN AMERICA

EUGENE DEBS IS the radical of Marguerite Young's title, but the special pleasures of *Harp Song for a Radical* flow from its vast and bizarre cast of supporting characters.[1] Debs has barely been introduced before we are whisked off to Europe to meet the German poet Heinrich Heine, Karl Marx, and assorted utopian mystics. At book's end, 580 pages later, we are in Russia with Fyodor Dostoevsky, whose death sentence has been commuted at the last possible moment.

Along the way the widow Mary Todd Lincoln, crossing the Atlantic, is saved by Sarah Bernhardt from a bad fall; the angel Moroni directs Joseph Smith to the gold tablets that will become the Mormon Bible. Mark Twain tries to read it and pronounces it "chloroform in print." We are introduced to Susan Anthony's mother, "poor creature," exhausted by childbearing, who "wished many times to die as she saw [her husband] approach with the love light burning in his eyes."

Edward A. Hannegan, an Indiana politician, becomes ambassador to Prussia, bows "to kiss the blushing hand of the fair queen," thus rousing her jealous husband to such "absolute rage and horror" that he sends Hannegan back to the Wabash, "his whole life wrecked." Hannegan decides to seek the presidency so he can get revenge by

---

1. *Harp Song for a Radical: The Life and Times of Eugene Victor Debs* (Knopf, 2000).

making war on Prussia, only to wreck his life again by murdering his brother-in-law in a drunken rage. Tears splash down the "granite cheeks" of Woodrow Wilson when he hears that James Whitcomb Riley, author of *Little Orphant Annie*, is dead.

Just when it seems that the book will cram in everybody but Uncle Tom Cobbleigh and Whistler's mother, who should appear on page 546 but "a stiffly corseted . . . Bible thumper of an evangelical reformist spirit"? That's right: it's Whistler's mother handing out religious tracts in Russia. Accompanying Whistler's father on a railroad-building job for the tsar, she is trying to save the Russian Orthodox soul by distributing printed matter with "Simple Simon Bible truth, American style, the text in Russian so simple that not only a Russian serf but a Russian muley cow might understand" it.

People who love stories ought to be delighted with this book. If you are a crusty stick-in-the-mud about historical precision, you are more likely to ask, "What kind of book is this anyhow?" It isn't what now passes for biography, which usually means every inconsequential fact a writer can find to inflate a fifty-page life into a six-hundred-page doorstop. Nor is it history in the sense that finicky historians think of history.

Here's the kind of book it is:

On page 391, Ohio's distinguished political family, the Harrisons, who gave us "Old Tippecanoe" and President Benjamin too, are burying old Congressman John Scott Harrison when they notice that the grave of his recently interred young nephew looks "as if it had been trampled over by a drove of long-snouted hogs." Suspicion points to agents of a "capitalism extended beyond normal procedures"; to wit, a grave robber, some "resurrectionist" employed to provide educational materials for a medical school.

> While searching for the [dead nephew] at the Cincinnati Medical College, which had a back alley where mysterious wagons were known to slide down a coal chute bags which were not bags of

coal, General Ben Harrison's brother John and a constable had drawn up a windlass from the bottom of a shaft . . . not the body of the young man who was their quarry but, as had been seen by the policeman when he lifted the mask from his face, an old man. It was the body of the former congressman who had been drawn up and whose startled son had stared into his face with the cry—"My God! My father!"

Where do all these stories come from? It is impossible to tell. The book hasn't a single footnote. While the stories are fascinating—those tears splashing down Wilson's granite cheeks!—one inevitably wonders about their provenance. How did Young know how Susan Anthony's mother felt when her husband approached in amorous fettle? Is there a memoir? An old letter perhaps? This is not a book for those needing facts they can take into court.

Fussy English majors will also fret. Young's sentences meander on for 150, 200, 250 words while tenses shift quixotically and pronouns wander around with no antecedents. Now and then the reader becomes lost inside a mammoth sentence that has no verb to reveal what it intended to say when it embarked on its journey. Here and there, other sentences must be reread, then reread again to make them give up their message.

There are metaphors galore, not all of them felicitous. Thus: The Ohio River "moved as slowly as a flight of pregnant, large-bellied mares with a tossing foam of curls as it neighed with inflated nostrils between the Ohio and Kentucky shores." And, after the death of Karl Marx's son Edgar, "there never would be another son who was the fruit of Mrs. Marx's loins. . . . Over the door to Mrs. Marx's womb a funeral wreath of pale winter leaves with black and red ribbons might just as well have been laid."

Defects and eccentricities are normal in an unfinished manuscript, and Marguerite Young's book is clearly unfinished. When she died in

1995, she hadn't yet done the polishing, revising, and rewriting required for a finished manuscript. More seriously, although the life of Eugene Victor Debs was to be at the center of things, her narrative had not reached his mature years. In this period Debs led labor in some of its most passionate struggles with industry, formed an American Socialist Party and the International Workers of the World, went to prison as a war resister, and twice received a surprisingly big vote while running for president, once while serving time in a federal penitentiary. In these years he became a saintly figure for many who felt helpless against American capitalism at its most ruthless. Lacking the story of this period, Young's book doesn't end; it comes to a shuddering halt.

It is sobering to ponder how long it might have taken her to bring it to a graceful conclusion, for speedy composition was not her way. She wrote books of poetry and a study of American utopias but her only novel, *Miss MacIntosh, My Darling*, took twenty years to write. Nearly 1,200 pages long, it runs to some 675,000 words and was published in 1965.[2] At her death thirty years later she had still not published again.

Unfinished though her *Harp Song* is, and often quirky, its aim is heroic. Young was trying to produce a sort of unified-field theory of nineteenth-century political history. She seems to believe that the radical political movements that aroused laborers and farmers after the Civil War flowed from the same utopian impulse that brought dreamers bearing "strange faiths" from Europe in the pre-war years. Twenty years before the Civil War, utopianism had spread from the Atlantic ports of entry deep into the Middle West. Believers in salvation through celibacy mingled with political theorists dreaming of "a universal Jesusville made of socialists only." There were Saint-Simonians, Millerites, Shakers, and Rappites. Young describes a New York swarming in the 1840s with

---

2. Reissued by Dalkey Archive Press, 1993.

radicals of every breed who seemed permanently amazed by the utopian prospects that seemed to be opening in this millennial land.... There were utopian philosophers of every kind mixing with clowns, politicians, confidence men.... There were scriptural communists with secular dreams prompted by mystical origins as there were followers of Robert Owen, Charles Fourier, Etienne Cabet of the Icarians, Brisbaneites, Perfectionists who were believers in society's reform, whether immediate, as if by sudden transfiguration, or remote.

Young Walt Whitman, covering a convention of radical dreamers for the *Brooklyn Eagle*, couldn't decide whether to dismiss it as "humbug" or "commend it as containing the germ of a bold though fruitless inquiry into the wrongs and evils of the world." Since God had not seen fit to make the world pure and perfect, Whitman thought it unlikely that Robert Owen could do so. Later, though, Whitman thought again. Perhaps he had seen

a vision, however far off, of the relation existing between all men as members of one great family; the duty and pleasure of loving and helping one the other; the dwelling together of the nations in peace...bound together by the ties of a common brotherhood.

Fascinated by the utopians and their communities, Young celebrates several of the more obscure at great length. We learn more than many may care to know, for instance, about the German "socialist utopian peddler" Wilhelm Weitling and his Iowa commune, Kolonie Kommunia. It failed quickly. Most utopias did. Then, as now, most Americans were more interested in making money than in the unlikely probability of earthly paradise. Sometimes public indifference turned to outright violence, as when Joseph Smith, the founder of Mormonism, was lynched in Illinois in what amounted to a conspiracy of the best people to get the Mormons out of town.

Yet Mormonism produced the only utopian success. Whether modern Utah is an earthly paradise may be debatable, but Young includes Mormon doctrine in her catalog of utopian dreams. Not reluctant to offend present-day Mormons, she treats the story of the church's origin as a crackpot tale probably rooted in hoax. Telling the familiar story of Joseph Smith, "the divinely inflated but secular many-colored utopian prophet," being visited by the angel Moroni, she reports that the angel's appearance occurred while Smith was "lying in his bed, perhaps under the spell of imbibing more of the blood-red wine than he should have imbibed." Young's retelling of the story goes like this:

The angel told of a hidden book, product of a religion long lost to earth, written in strange tongues on gold plates. Smith found the plates. They were taken to his father-in-law's farmhouse, where Smith lived. Later, asked who had brought them, Smith said they had been hidden in a bag of wheat delivered by the mailman. "The angel Moroni in disguise," Young suggests. The father-in-law, however, said the bag contained no wheat, nothing but clothing: shirts, pants, underwear.

Found with the "phenomenal, superphenomenal" plates of gold were two stones which Smith called Urim and Thummim. These he used as decoders—"spiritual spectacles"—to help him translate the ancient writing. Martin Harris, a well-to-do farmer, helped Smith with the translating and underwrote publication of what became the Book of Mormon. When questions arose about the authenticity of the gold plates, they conveniently disappeared. Martin Harris, saying his wife didn't believe they existed, had nagged Smith to let him take them home to show her. Smith finally agreed, the plates went to Harris's house, and Mrs. Harris lost them. If the explanation sounds ridiculous, Young clearly meant it to.

Her respect for Brigham Young, by contrast, produces some of her most lyrical writing. Here the Mormons are preparing to start their magnificent trek to the West:

> When...it became apparent that Brigham Young was preparing to leave, for he and his Mormon followers had gathered the last crop of the pale winter wheat and had not sown another crop, and all that they had built up together had been lost by forced sale or had been abandoned when there was no buyer at any price for the beehive that could not be transported by wagon so that the beehive people would have to produce another hive in which to spin the honey of the sun—they knew not where—he who was preparing with the majority of his followers to cross the Mississippi in this darkest time of the year had heard from one of his disciples that it did seem a pity they should have to leave the beautiful and not quite completed edifice which was the temple to the moon and the sun, had answered that yes, it was beautiful. "But we have the satisfaction of taking the substance with us, leaving behind us only the shadow."

The trouble with Marguerite Young's long, entertaining romp through Mormon history is that it has nothing to do with what appears to be her book's theme; that is, that the gentle utopianism of the 1840s spawned the violent confrontation between labor and capital after the Civil War. She simply can't resist stopping everything to tell a good story, regardless of its pertinence. As a result, you gradually become so engrossed in her stories that you cease caring about her argument, or whether she is even making an argument.

We read of Heinrich Heine dreaming about his dead father, and rushing to kiss his hand, only to find that the fingers he kissed were dry twigs and his father himself a leafless tree covered with frost. What this has to do with utopianism and radicalism is hard to see, but the poetry of it is lovely. Here is some arresting and irrelevant gossip about the Russian tsar Paul I. He was rumored to have come to the family dinner table wearing the imperial crown of the Romanovs. And when he "spoke of chopping off a row of heads as lightly as if they were the plumes of dandelions," he seemed to have his children in mind. As tidbits like this roll forth, it is tempting simply to relax, enjoy the landscape, and let Young's thesis take care of itself. In any case, it is never very persuasive.

When her story shifts from the 1840 utopians to the conspicuous consumers of the Gilded Age, a more plausible explanation emerges for the outburst of radicalism that would affect American politics far into the twentieth century. It is this: "The moneyed interests"—Justice Holmes's delicate term for capitalists who had triumphed in the Civil War—behaved with such selfishness, such arrogance, such brutality, and such contempt for the new industrial workforce that uprisings were inevitable. When they occurred, workers invariably found their causes crushed by the new monarchs of coal, steel, rails, and oil working in alliance with every arm of government. The president might order the army to intervene in a strike. Restoring order was the usual justification, but the order to be restored was always the order of "the moneyed interests."

Governors provided National Guard units for strikebreaking duty, sometimes only after the struck company agreed to pay the bill. Courts genially issued orders for workers to stop misbehaving and genially fined or imprisoned those who didn't obey. Even God was on the side of big money. The Reverend Henry Ward Beecher told his well-heeled flock: "God has intended the great to be great and the little to be little. No equalization process can ever take place until men are made equal as productive forces. It is a wild vision, not a practicable theory."

Big money's arrogance was eloquently expressed in Henry C. Frick's comment after the bloody crushing of the Homestead steel strike in 1892: "We had to teach our employees a lesson and we taught them one they will never forget." The judge advocate of the Colorado National Guard, called to break up a mining strike in 1902, dismissed questions about the constitutionality of his mission: "To hell with the Constitution; we are not following the Constitution!" When the union filed habeas corpus pleas for release of its members, the commander of the guard units said, "Habeas corpus be damned, we'll give 'em post mortems!"

This was the time of Vernon Louis Parrington's "great barbecue," when sympathetic politicians parceled out the nation's wealth in a "splendid feast...Gargantuan in its rough plenty." Rich and poor did not fare equally well at the table, however. The Homestead Act, to be sure, gave the homesteader 160 acres of land at $1.25 per acre, but the Union Pacific land grant gave its promoters an entire empire for nothing.

In the decades that followed, Parrington wrote, "there was to be no bargaining with corporations for the use of what the public gave; they took what they wanted and no impertinent questions were asked."

In *The Rise of American Civilization*, their classic 1927 survey of American history, Charles and Mary Beard treat the excesses of the age as a historical inevitability. The pattern of rich businessmen over-powering agricultural societies could be traced from the most ancient of times up through the imperial Romans to the triumph of the French and English business class over their landed aristocracies. Where Young sees a villainous industrial despotism in the new age, the Beards see a familiar story of

> aggressive men, akin in spirit to military captains of the past, working their way up from the ranks, exploiting natural resources without restraint, waging economic war on one another, entering into combinations, making immense fortunes, and then, like successful feudal chieftains or medieval merchants, branching out as patrons of learning, divinity, and charity.

Young's view is not so measured. She insists repeatedly that the most important result of the Civil War was to split the country into two houses: "the house of the few rich and the house of the many poor with the abyss widening between them." She is fond of hissing villains and has a long list of them. The abuse with which she heaps them, if sometimes unfair, expresses a loathing so passionate that it is exhilarating to read in these days of bland and bloodless political writing. What we have here is good old-fashioned radical bile directed at what Harry Truman used to call "the special interests." Nowadays, when political discourse is limited to exalting material excess and the acquisitive instinct, it is as startling as a cold shower in January.

Young's roll of villains is not limited to the usual suspects like Frick, Gould, Pullman, Fisk, Harriman, and Presidents Hayes, Harrison, and Cleveland. Among its surprises we find John Hay, for instance, once Lincoln's secretary. She despises him for, among other things, living on Euclid Avenue in Cleveland. It was a street populated with

> American despots who lived in an atmosphere of Medici magnificence, the coal and iron and steel and oil barons... [who] were undergoing or had already undergone the aurification which permitted them to wield unholy powers over the lives and deaths of poor men, but which did not arouse the outraged moral disapproval of Old Dirty Socks Abe Lincoln's former secretary....

There are eighty words still to come in this sentence, but no clue whether "Old Dirty Socks" is Hay or Lincoln.

She is merciless on Lincoln's son Robert, partly because she thinks he treated his widowed mother badly, partly because of legal services he performed for George Pullman, the sleeping-car tycoon. "The Prince of Nails," as she calls the Emancipator's son, "would drive the nails into his possibly mad and possibly sane mother's already broken heart and would be the lawyer for...the despot Pullman and would drive the nails into Debs's heart and crucify his labor union as surely as if he were nailing it up on a mound of burning cinders in a railroad yard."

It is Allan Pinkerton, however, who fascinates her. She spends eighty or ninety pages on Pinkerton, his sons, the Pinkerton detective James McParlan, and the Molly Maguires who terrorized the Pennsylvania anthracite fields. McParlan made the legal case that finally sent thirty men to the gallows. Whether they were the men who had actually committed the specific crimes attributed to the Molly Maguires was not entirely certain, but the court was not so interested in certainty as it was in crushing a threat to the safety and success of the mine owners.

This is a terrible and gripping story, and Young tells it well. Pinkerton, who created a private police force to serve American industry, had been a radical Chartist agitator in Scotland and fled Glasgow with a price on his head. In Chicago he underwent transformation from refugee political radical to America's most effective, most feared, and most hated "detective." An "antilabor detective," Young calls him, not unjustly.

The Molly Maguires were a secretive, closed society of Irish immigrants who, as Young tells it, had come to Pennsylvania's anthracite region before the Civil War "in search of survival." They had been embittered by the Civil War draft law, she writes, when they were "dragged from the coal pits and tied hand and foot, slung like corpses over horses or tied by ropes and dragged along the ground to the draft headquarters for shipment to the southern battlefields."

Most Irish immigrants of their time had fled to America to escape starvation and the tyranny of absentee English landlords. They had no enthusiasm for being pressed into the Union Army to face death for a cause that was utterly meaningless to them. It was especially galling to learn that people with money could buy their way out of the war by paying substitutes to fill their uniforms. To a newly arrived immigrant it looked like a war in which the stay-at-home rich profited from the death of the poor.

And so the Irish miners in Pennsylvania after the war lacked a sense of piety toward American justice. These were men whose people for generations had waged a silent guerrilla warfare against English landlords, and they brought this history with them to Pennsylvania. When wages fell as coal profits rose, sullen resentment developed into an outraged sense of injustice, then into fury, then into acts of desperation. Murders and violent assaults began to occur.

Suspicion fell on the secretive Molly Maguires. The mine owners retained Pinkerton; Pinkerton's man McParlan infiltrated the Irish community and came out with evidence to take to court. Convictions came easily. Twenty men were hanged after the first trial, ten more during the next two years. Thanks to Pinkerton and McParlan, the mine owners had brought the ultimate peace to the anthracite fields.

Young's account of all this concedes that the Molly Maguires engaged in "the assassination of repressive railroad barons and railroad owners and coal-mine barons and their sycophantic bosses." But had McParlan's detective work uncovered the real killers? She gives an emphatic no. The men the state hanged were "sacrificial scapegoats" and their execution "the archetypal crime of capital against labor," she asserts without, alas, citing evidence.

In Young's turmoil of expressionistic history, we often lose sight of Eugene Debs. His parents were Alsatian French. His father, well educated and fond of literature, named him Eugene Victor after his favorite writers, the novelists Eugène Sue and Victor Hugo.

Debs was born in Terre Haute, Indiana, in 1855, where his parents ran a small grocery. He was bright in school but quit at age fourteen to work on the railroad. It was 1870, Grant was president, and the heroic age of the railroad had just begun. Debs never lost his love of it. He began as a helper in the paint shop, then became a locomotive fireman, working up in the cab with the engineer, feeding coal into the boiler. Could he truly have read Plato's *Republic* while keeping a locomotive boiler fired? Young says he did.

Losing his job in the depression of the 1870s, he found work in St. Louis, where he was shocked to find that "the rich danced under twelve hundred tons of crystal chandeliers in halls of gold-framed mirrors and the poor lived in hog hovels." Back in Indiana, he worked as a billing clerk in a grocery warehouse, but love of railroading drew him to the freight yards in his idle hours. There he fell in with Joshua Leach, who was recruiting members for the Brotherhood of Locomotive Firemen. Debs enlisted, impressed Leach, and at age twenty-three became editor of *The Locomotive Firemen's Magazine*.

Railroading was dangerous work. Dreadful wrecks happened with appalling regularity. Railroad men were scalded to death by steam, crushed when locomotives fell through poorly built bridges, and mutilated when badly laid track flew apart and sent trains tumbling down embankments. Debs filled the magazine with stories of railroaders killed and crippled; he became interested in politics and discovered he had a talent for it. He made his first speech at age twenty-three. He was city clerk of Terre Haute before he was thirty and went on to serve a term in the state legislature. There, after his proposals for women's suffrage and railroad safety legislation were overwhelmingly beaten, he concluded that no significant reforms could be achieved by conventional politics. Late in life, having gone twice to prison, he remarked that he had once "permitted myself to be elected to a state legislature" and was "as much ashamed of that as I am of having gone to jail."

Young's history doesn't reach his mature years, in which he became a charismatic leader of the union movement, created the powerful American Railway Union, and saw it busted when he, foolishly perhaps, let it be drawn into the Pullman strike of 1894. With the help of President Cleveland, the railroad owners obtained a court injunction which essentially ordered the strike to cease. The ARU leaders voted to ignore the order. Debs was arrested, tried for contempt of court without a jury, convicted, and sentenced to six months in prison. His union was destroyed.

Seeing labor crushed by a government in alliance with business, Debs moved toward socialism, saying, "I am for Socialism because I am for humanity. We have been cursed with the reign of gold long enough." As the presidential candidate of his new Social Democratic Party, Debs polled 96,000 votes in 1900. In 1904, his vote rose to 402,000. Socialism that year called for minimum wages, a maximum on work hours, women's suffrage, and abolition of child labor. Though these issues have long since been appropriated by the major parties and enacted, they were the very essence of crackpot, possibly dangerous radicalism in 1904.

In 1912 Debs polled 901,000 votes, 6 percent of the national total in an election that also had William Howard Taft, Woodrow Wilson, and Theodore Roosevelt on the ballot.

Opposition to the First World War brought him afoul of Wilson, who had once been the champion of peace, but who by 1917 was in war mode, as modern political lingo might phrase it. Under Wilson's stewardship, a patriotic hysteria was being created in support of a war to make the world safe for democracy. The Espionage Act was interpreted to mean that opposing the war was criminal, and Debs opposed it openly as an instrument that would enrich "the master class" at the expense of "the subject class."

"The master class has always declared the wars; the subject class has always fought the battles," he said. "The master class has had all to gain and nothing to lose, while the subject class has had nothing to gain and all to lose." He was promptly charged with violating the Espionage Act, sentenced to ten years in prison, and sent to the maximum security penitentiary in Atlanta. A sentence to Atlanta was hard time, and Debs served three years of it. By 1920 he was frail and ailing. Wilson's attorney general, fearing it would embarrass the government if Debs died in prison, advised Wilson to set him free.

Debs seems to have had a remarkable sweetness of character that made people love him, but Wilson was not easily seduced. Wilson was a man of high principle. He rejected clemency, saying, "This man was a traitor to his country and will never be pardoned during my administration." The sentence was commuted by Warren Harding in 1921 after his attorney general, Harry Daugherty, having interviewed Debs, told Clarence Darrow, "I never met a man I liked better."

It is hard to explain the affection so many felt for Eugene Debs. Nowadays we take it for granted that a lovable politician is a fraudulent creation of public relations artists and ghostwriters. Debs, though, was the genuine article. James Whitcomb Riley, the Hoosier Wordsworth, tried to explain it in verse:

> And there's Gene Debs—a man 'at stands
> And jes' holds out in his two hands
> As warm a heart as ever beat
> Betwixt here and the Jedgement Seat!

In *U.S.A.*, John Dos Passos etched a portrait of Debs titled "Lover of Mankind":

> He was a tall shamblefooted man,
> had a sort of gusty rhetoric that
> set on fire the railroad workers in
> their pine-boarded halls
>
> made them want the world he wanted,
> a world brothers might own
> where everybody would split even...

Chapter 4

FEUD

IN THE TIME of Lyndon Johnson's vice-presidential agony I found myself one day in his Capitol office listening to a Johnson soliloquy. Its central theme was his devotion to John F. Kennedy, but there were several lesser motifs. When Johnson was launched on one of these meditations, torrents of words poured out of him. On this occasion he canvassed the spectrum from the magisterial arrogance of Charles de Gaulle, to poverty in India, to his youthful career as a rural Texas schoolteacher. Always, however, the talk came back to his admiration for President Kennedy.

Johnson knew me only as a nameless face in the press gallery. In the middle of the monologue he surreptitiously, without interrupting the word flow, sent a note out to his secretary asking, "Who is this I'm talking to?" He was performing for an audience of one, and that one a stranger, but he probably thought some of it might just possibly turn up in a newspaper, and he was making it plain what the headline should say: Lyndon Johnson Utterly Devoted to John F. Kennedy.

To hear him tell it, there had never been a happier second banana. Never mind that the Kennedys had humiliated him when he tried for the presidential nomination in 1960. Never mind that the Kennedys' glittering young courtiers—the "Harvards," as Johnson called them

—joked constantly and cruelly about him. Never mind that the press was calling him a forlorn figure who no longer mattered.

Never mind realities. On this day, playing to a nameless Capitol reporter, he spoke of the vice-presidential life as a friendship with a man he admired extravagantly. He told a story, not necessarily fictional, of an intimate dinner for three—Johnson, the President, and Jackie—in the Kennedys' private White House quarters. Mrs. Kennedy had told him how greatly she and Jack needed him, how thankful they were for his help in lightening the presidential burden.

There was a tribute to the steely strength with which President Kennedy dispatched his enemies. He, Johnson, had experienced that cruel but manly strength himself when running against Jack for the nomination in 1960. He admired the way Jack had disposed of him so coolly, so dispassionately, without softness or irresolution.

My notes of this bizarre talk had quotation marks around the words "when he looks you straight in the eye and puts that knife into you without flinching...." This was Johnson's metaphor for what Kennedy had done to him at the convention in Los Angeles. One was supposed to believe that Johnson now admired him for it.

It seemed doubtful that he truly admired Kennedy's cool way with the knife. He was too proud, too vain, too thin-skinned. More likely, it still hurt so much that he couldn't stop talking about it. It seemed probable that such a man who had been subjected to such an ordeal might bear a grudge for the rest of his life.

Praise John Kennedy to one and all though he did, Johnson had reasons to feel less than enchanted about their relationship. Here was greatness comically humbled. As Senate leader, Johnson had been the marvel of Washington. His mastery of the Senate amounted to genius, or so it was said by the Washington crowd, so quick to adore today's hero, so ready to call him a chump tomorrow. "The second most powerful man in Washington," the press had called him.

And what had John Kennedy done in Johnson's Senate? He had been a mostly absent backbencher: an affable young fellow, to be sure, but rarely seen at the Capitol, not one to be taken seriously except for his father's wealth. Everyone knew the old man was grooming Jack to be president, and real senators, serious men, the big mules, disdained senators whose presidential ambitions showed. "Always running for president," they said of such men, with amused contempt.

Several senators were running for president in the 1950s, Lyndon Johnson among them, though he pretended almost to the end that he wasn't. If you had the itch, good Senate form forbade you to let it show too early. Kennedy was something new. He didn't care about good Senate form. By 1960 he had been running shamelessly and vigorously for four years. Real power in America lay in the White House, not in the Senate, he told anybody who bothered to ask why he was running. And of course, he was also being a dutiful son, trying to realize his father's grandiose dream of putting a son in the presidency.

Johnson played a trickier hand. He was the conscientious statesman sticking to his job, doing his sweaty duty in Washington while Kennedy toured the landscape chasing the presidency. Johnson answered the quorum calls, shepherded the good bills to passage, killed the bad bills in their tracks, labored tirelessly for the nation's good. He was being responsible. "Responsible" became a popular word among his camp followers. Johnson was betting that his dazzling senatorial skills would awe enough Democratic convention delegates to win him the nomination. It showed his profound ignorance of national party politics.

It was Kennedy who had it right. He let Johnson worry about the quorum calls and traveled the country courting local party captains; fighting in primaries and state conventions; jawboning governors, mayors, and union leaders, twisting their arms when necessary. If you seemed terribly young, it didn't hurt to show you were a little tough.

He and brother Bobby and a passionately dedicated organization with seemingly unlimited financing cultivated the working politicians who constituted the party machinery. Johnson didn't. The Kennedys made mincemeat of him.

There was an impromptu debate at the convention. Johnson talked of his tireless service in the Senate. Kennedy scarcely talked at all. He and Johnson had no disagreements on policy matters, he said, so the sensible thing would be for the party to put him in the White House and keep Lyndon in the Senate meeting those quorum calls. He sat down. The audience laughed, and Johnson was finished. Without flinching, Kennedy had put that knife into him.

Did Johnson secretly dislike Jack Kennedy? Not likely. It was impossible for almost anyone to feel a personal dislike for Jack Kennedy. What Johnson did dislike was the culture Kennedy represented.

The full Kennedy package—complete with Kennedys, advisors, thinkers, speechwriters, professors, press cheerleaders, advance men, sycophants, and gofers—came bearing a sense of its own intellectual superiority. They had been to the best colleges, Harvard being the school of preference, and they were not slow to let you know they were an intellectual and cultural elite. The style was cool, polished, urbane. They admired wit and understatement. The women had finishing school poise; the men favored muted pinstripes and buttoned-down collars. Most shared a feeling that the Kennedys were an entitled people.

They represented a culture that had been detested and feared in the South and West for a century. They looked not too different from the citified, hard-money crowd that William Jennings Bryan had once accused of crucifying the nation upon a cross of gold. Johnson's political idol, Sam Rayburn, had long memories of New York and Boston moneymen squeezing the South and West to the edge of bankruptcy. Later Johnson's presidency, far more liberal than Kennedy's had been, would reveal how deeply his politics were rooted in the Populist movement of the nineteenth century.

So there were very old regional antipathies at work between Johnson and the Kennedys: rural populism versus Northeastern establishment. It wouldn't have mattered if President Kennedy had lived. Johnson would simply have disappeared. A Johnson with presidential power might be more liberal than Kennedy, but he was still hard for the Kennedy culture to accept. They were contemptuous of him, as the hard-money Democrats of the Northeast had once been contemptuous of the rustic Bryan. Late in his presidency Johnson complained bitterly and often of the Northeasterners' attitude.

"I always knew that the greatest bigots in the world lived in the East, not the South," he told Richard Goodwin. "Economic bigots, social bigots, society bigots. Whatever I did, they were bound to think it was some kind of trick. How could some politician from Johnson City do what was right for the country?"

To Johnson, the Kennedy who represented everything hateful about the Northeast was Jack's brother Robert, known to the public as "Bobby." Bobby, in turn, saw Johnson as an unprincipled, lying yahoo. He ignored or insulted him as Jack's vice president and, after the assassination, hated him as a usurper of Jack's rightful power. The result was a personal feud that poisoned the Democratic Party for most of the 1960s.

Mutual Contempt is an exhaustive and fascinating history of this nasty quarrel, which Jeff Shesol has assembled from the mountain of existing documents, books, and oral histories about the Kennedys and Johnson, and interviews of his own.[1] Some of his freshest material comes from documents just now becoming available at the Johnson Library in Austin, including taped recordings of LBJ's White House phone conversations.

Another valuable new book culled from the Johnson Library is

---

1. *Mutual Contempt: Lyndon Johnson, Robert Kennedy, and the Feud That Defined a Decade* (Norton, 1997).

Lyndon B. Johnson's Vietnam Papers, edited by David M. Barrett.[2] This is a generous collection of White House documents recording Johnson's stubborn march to his doom. Since Bobby Kennedy was a major opponent of LBJ's Vietnam policy, the Barrett collection is a valuable supplement to *Mutual Contempt*.

Shesol was twenty-eight years old when he wrote his book. Not born until after the Johnson–Kennedy feud was long over, he is happily unencumbered by the prejudices of many still alive who were devoted to one or the other. The result is a remarkably evenhanded telling of a story that still makes many an old-timer's blood boil. Having watched it from afar with no personal stake in the outcome, I think he gets it just about right.

Perhaps he is slightly off the beat about the Vietnam phase of the thing. He magnifies unduly the Bobby factor in Johnson's decision not to run for reelection; early Senate doves like Fulbright, Church, Morse, and Gruening get short shrift, and Eugene McCarthy's importance is almost entirely ignored. Richard Nixon's role in undermining Johnson's war policy is never mentioned. The fury of the great national debate that brought Johnson down gets lost in the smaller story of two of Bobby's aides, Adam Walinsky and Peter Edelman, futilely trying to make him challenge Johnson on Vietnam.

For the most part, though, Shesol's grasp of the era's history is sure, his tale often entertaining, and his research impressive. Perhaps too much so for the casual reader. With books getting longer and longer these days, 475 pages may be tolerable for a good story like this about a minor historical spat. Still, one yearns for the pre-computer age when the laborious demands of typewriters and coldhearted editors held such books down to 250 pages carrying the reader rapidly from cover to cover.

---

2. *Lyndon B. Johnson's Vietnam Papers: A Documentary Collection* (Texas A&M University Press, 1997).

Shesol's narrative has four stages: (1) Bobby's opposition to Johnson at the 1960 Democratic Convention, (2) Johnson's refusal to make Bobby his vice-presidential candidate in 1964, (3) Bobby's establishing a power base in New York from which to build a 1972 presidential campaign, and (4) Johnson's self-destruction and Bobby's decision to go for the presidency in 1968.

The Johnson–Bobby hostilities opened at the 1960 Democratic Convention in Los Angeles. John Kennedy asked Johnson to come on the ticket. Why is disputed. Bobby opposed the choice. Johnson surprised almost everybody by accepting. Bobby let everybody know he hated having Johnson on the ticket. Everybody included Johnson. Four years later LBJ would have the pleasure of denying Bobby the vice-presidential nomination on the 1964 ticket. (This irritating Washington custom of calling the gods by their nicknames, deplorable though it be, helps avoid a baffling confusion of Kennedys.)

Bobby was angry on several scores. One was Johnson's eleventh-hour try for the nomination in 1960 after telling the Kennedys he would not run. Another was Johnson's collusion in a scheme to stampede the convention galleries for Adlai Stevenson. If Stevenson could be used to block Jack's nomination, the convention would turn to someone else, maybe Lyndon Johnson. Jack, the instinctive politician, took the relaxed view that all this was just part of the game. Bobby, a moralist who disliked politicians, saw only a double cross.

Worst of all for Bobby, Johnson agents were raising troubling questions about Jack's health. On the eve of the convention, India Edwards publicly declared that Kennedy had Addison's disease and "would not be alive today if it were not for cortisone."

"Malicious and false," Bobby immediately replied. Obviously referring to Johnson, he said there were some Democrats who, "if they cannot win the nomination themselves,...want the Democrat who does win to lose in November."

In fact, Kennedy did have Addison's disease and was indeed

dependent on cortisone, but Convention Eve was no time for the beguiling Kennedy candor. "Smiling broadly, boasting of his own 'vigor,'" Shesol writes, Kennedy managed to "blithely outlast the mud-slinging which he regarded as part of the game of politics." Jack was a good politician, Bobby wasn't. "Unlike Jack," Shesol writes, "Bobby blamed Lyndon Johnson." He tells a story from Bobby Baker, Johnson's closest Senate aide, about seeing Bobby Kennedy at breakfast in the Los Angeles Biltmore:

> When Baker suggested mildly that Ted Kennedy had been perhaps "a bit rough" in suggesting that Johnson had not fully recovered from his 1955 heart attack, Bobby Kennedy's face flushed red. "You've got your nerve," he snapped, clenching his fists, leaning forward threateningly. "Lyndon Johnson has compared my father to the Nazis and John Connally and India Edwards lied in saying my brother is dying of Addison's disease. You Johnson people are running a stinking damned campaign and you're going to get yours when the time comes!"

A day or two later what Johnson got was the vice-presidential nomination.

Shesol has a low opinion of Bobby the politician. "Bobby was more a moralist than an operator, better suited to criminal investigations than Capitol Hill intrigue. And unlike John Kennedy, who treated fellow politicians with affable indifference, Bobby wore his contempt openly.... Politics was the dirty business Bobby did for his brother. It was, Bobby later scoffed, 'a hell of a way to make a living.'"

In retrospect, when the election returns showed Kennedy had beaten Nixon by a split hair, Bobby's opposition to having Johnson on the ticket looked politically absurd. Without Johnson, Kennedy would almost certainly have lost Texas. Even with Johnson his Texas majority was only 50.5 percent. The ticket also carried six Southern states where Johnson's down-home accent sounded more appealing than Kennedy's high-velocity Bostonese.

There are many versions of how the Kennedy-Johnson ticket was created. David Barrett's *Vietnam Papers* records Johnson's, as told eight years later. In 1968, three days after announcing he would not run again, he met with Bobby at the White House. Bobby wanted to know if Johnson would now oppose him for the nomination. Johnson finessed the question by talking about everything else. Walt Rostow's notes of the conversation, included in Barrett's *Vietnam Papers*, show Johnson was still brooding on the ancient history of 1960:

> The President went on to say that in fact he had not wanted to be Vice President and had not wanted to be President. Two men had persuaded him to run in 1960: Sam Rayburn and Phil Graham [publisher of *The Washington Post*]. They had said that unless Johnson were on the ticket, John Kennedy could not carry the South. Without the South, Nixon would win. He would have greatly preferred to have continued to be the leader of the Senate.
>
> The Vice Presidency is a job that no one likes. It is inherently demeaning....

One can see history being converted to humbug here. If Johnson had not wanted to be president, why did he fight for the nomination in 1960? Had he really wanted to remain Senate leader instead of becoming vice president? Possibly. He had seen the "demeaning" side of the vice presidency in Franklin Roosevelt's treatment of another Texas vice president, "Cactus Jack" Garner, but he had also seen the vice presidency put Nixon in line for the White House. It is plausible that Rayburn and Graham were decisive in the matter. Whether they argued that only Johnson could carry the South no one else could truly say by 1968. Perhaps so. Or perhaps Johnson was adjusting history a bit to remind Bobby of how wrong he had been not to want

LBJ on the ticket. And of course, Johnson was also saying that the Kennedys were in his debt. It is unlikely Bobby agreed.

As vice president, Johnson got to know what "demeaning" was. President Kennedy "tolerated no word of disrespect," according to Shesol, but presidential will is often impossible to enforce. He put one of his closest aides, Kenneth O'Donnell, "in charge of the care and feeding of LBJ." It was a poor choice.

> O'Donnell was indifferent and offhandedly cruel.... Open disparagement of Johnson was rare, but O'Donnell's demeanor typified what Johnson's staff perceived as a "loose contempt" for the vice president by the White House staff.... O'Donnell's arrogant disregard conveyed one simple, gleeful fact to the vice president: "We're it and you're not." Robert Kennedy communicated as much when he barged in and interrupted Johnson's private meetings with the president, launching into what he considered to be far more important business without so much as a nod of apology to LBJ.

Hickory Hill, Bobby's estate in McLean, Virginia, was the social center for New Frontiersmen, whom Shesol calls "the Hickory Hill gang." At their parties, "Johnson jokes and Johnson stories were as inexhaustible as they were merciless.... Partygoers asked, 'Whatever happened to Lyndon?' But no one could forget the galling fact that LBJ was in John Kennedy's administration. He was, in their eyes, a gatecrasher, an anomaly, an embarrassment to the President, and a blight on the bright New Frontier."

The assassination occurred. The world turned upside down.

Johnson's accession was devastating to Bobby. Johnson feared Bobby's response from the very beginning. Long afterward when he'd left the White House, he said Bobby's decision to oppose him for the nomination in 1968 was "the final straw." Thus Shesol:

> The thing I feared from the first day of my Presidency was actually coming true. Robert Kennedy had openly announced his intention to reclaim the throne in the memory of his brother.

This may be nothing more than emotion recollected in tranquility, for everyone, but especially Bobby, was too shattered in those first few weeks to think Shakespearean thoughts of thrones lost and reclaimed. As Bobby slowly recovered, some in the Kennedy organization began a quiet campaign to make him Johnson's running mate in 1964. Press speculation pumped steam into the campaign, and Washington was soon quarreling about whether Johnson had a duty to put the murdered president's brother in the vice presidency. Opponents held that the campaign was asserting an arrogant Kennedy claim to a dynastic entitlement to high office.

The more interesting question was how Johnson would contrive to give Bobby the inevitable bad news. There was too much bad blood between them, too many old scores to settle. Bobby had been too candid about his contempt for Johnson. Johnson was not going to have him on the ticket, probably wouldn't have had him on the ticket anyhow, because he wasn't Johnson's kind of politician, wasn't a politician at all by Johnson's standards.

Johnson's genius for the devious produced a comically elaborate scheme for ending the Bobby boom. He announced that since no member of his Cabinet should be tainted by politics he would not choose any Cabinet member for the vice-presidential nomination. As attorney general, Bobby was a Cabinet member.

Johnson had him to the White House to explain that he could not let the purity of his Cabinet be stained by political involvements. Johnson later told reporters, "When I told him, he gulped."

The irony of Johnson's obscene and gaudy self-destruction is that he was guided by John Kennedy's closest advisors (McNamara, Bundy,

Rusk, Maxwell Taylor & Company) in a doomed attempt to fulfill John Kennedy's grandiose inaugural pledge:

> Let every nation know, whether it wishes us well or ill, that we shall pay any price, bear any burden, meet any hardship, support any friend, oppose any foe, to assure the survival and success of liberty.

As the end approached for Johnson, mired in Vietnam, he was discovering that, no, Americans would not pay any price, bear any burden, meet any hardship, and he didn't know how to make them. He didn't really know why he was there, and he didn't know how to shake free without incurring political catastrophe at home. Foreign affairs had always been his weak point, and now he seemed drained of imagination and inventiveness. His genius was for domestic affairs, but now his grasp of domestic affairs failed him completely. The public was turning against the war policy in astonishing force, and he didn't know how to deal with a public like that, a public on the edge of mutiny against a whole war. What had become of patriotism?

His experts, who had mostly been John Kennedy's experts, counseled more and more war. More bombing, more troop commitments, more American participation in Vietnamese battles. Eventually the bomb tonnage dropped on Vietnam exceeded the tonnage dropped by all World War Two combatants on each other. His foreign policy advisors urged him to remember Munich. If the West had stood up to Hitler at Munich, World War Two might have been averted. Unless we stood up to communism in Vietnam...

What's more, he was not going to be the first president to lose a war. He escalated, and escalated again. Death piled up around him, and still he plunged ahead, powerless to conceive of a way out. A pullout would bring out the Nixon Republicans crying about a Democratic surrender to communism. He'd lived through the brutal

Republican campaigns charging Democrats with "twenty years of treason." Nixon had been a leader in that pack, and Nixon was still out there itching to pounce.

The further irony is that Robert F. Kennedy should have played such an important role in finishing off this stubbornly faithful champion of his brother's heroic rhetoric. Turmoil over Vietnam, a generational change, national fatigue with the cold war itself—something had become fundamentally different in the country. Johnson didn't seem to sense it. If he did, he was powerless to respond to it. Bobby Kennedy seemed at times to sense something new in the political air, but he too was slow to respond. He had got himself elected senator from New York to secure a power base for a presidential campaign. But he was thinking of 1972. Obedient to the rules of the old politics, he thought it would be fatal to challenge a sitting president of his own party.

So he let his opportunity pass, and, early in 1968, with Johnson's strength crumbling, Eugene McCarthy took it. Bobby's younger advisers, who sensed the change taking place in their own generation, had urged and urged him to take on Johnson in 1968. He made some speeches disagreeing with the Vietnam policy, but his own thinking on Vietnam was still hawkish. The nub of it was that instead of bombing, we should be using counterinsurgency forces. Neither man seemed to understand that the Vietnamese were fighting a war for independence.

In March, McCarthy's vote in the New Hampshire primary was big enough to show that LBJ was terribly weak. Worse for Johnson, McCarthy seemed likely to win the forthcoming primary in Minnesota, his home state. With the news of McCarthy's New Hampshire showing, Bobby jumped at last. It was late, terribly late, maybe too late. It was McCarthy who had won the devotion of the young who should have been Bobby's natural constituency. Many now regarded Bobby as a spoiler who had been too timid to fight against the odds, as McCarthy had. In consequence, Bobby was forced to fight McCarthy in a series of divisive primary elections. He had just won one when he was murdered in Los Angeles, for no apparent reason, by a Palestinian.

Rostow's notes of the conversation between LBJ and Bobby three days after Johnson withdrew from the 1968 campaign say:

> He wants Senator Kennedy to know he doesn't hate him, he doesn't dislike him, and that he still regards himself as carrying out the Kennedy/Johnson partnership.

Shesol thinks otherwise. "Kennedy did not fear Johnson," he concludes, "Johnson feared Kennedy, and hated him for it." He leaves no doubt that Kennedy hated Johnson to the very end.

Chapter 5

BRAVEST AND BEST

1.

WHEN THE ISRAELITES fled Egypt, God parted the waters of the sea and went before them in the form of a cloud to show them the way and of a pillar of fire to light their path by night. So says Exodus. *Parting the Waters* was the title of Volume One of Taylor Branch's huge, sprawling history of the civil rights movement, published in 1989. Now we have Volume Two, titled *Pillar of Fire*.[1]

What Branch wants us to take from these biblical titles is fairly obvious, I think. Among black Christians the story of Israel's captivity in Egypt always spoke eloquently of their own situation in the United States. They had been brought in chains, sold as chattels, and condemned to generations of forced servitude. One of their songs familiar even to whites was a lament for a people "way down in Egypt's land, oppressed so hard they could not stand." Its refrain, "Let my people go," paraphrased God's instruction to Moses: "Tell old Pharaoh, 'Let my people go.'"

Egypt's land when the civil rights movement began was the United States. A century after Lincoln, inhuman treatment was still the daily experience of black Americans. In this American Egypt, old Pharaoh

---

1. *Pillar of Fire: America in the King Years, 1963–1965* (Simon and Schuster, 1998).

was no single human being, but an interlocked network of white authority figures. These ranged from the president and Congress of the United States to the FBI's national police apparatus down through local school boards and church officers all the way to backwater Dixie's white-sheet set and decadent courts routinely excusing white thugs for murder. The Ku Klux Klan flourished, and not only in the South. Branch describes a Klan cross-burning ceremonial in St. Augustine, Florida, where the crowd was addressed by "a traveling celebrity Klansman" from California, the Reverend Connie Lynch, founder of the National States Rights Party. Four black girls had just been killed by a Sunday church bomber in Birmingham.

> ...Lynch dismissed squeamishness about the Birmingham church bombing, saying the four young girls had been "old enough to have venereal diseases" and were no more human or innocent than rattlesnakes. "So I kill 'em all," he shouted, "and if it's four less niggers tonight, then good for whoever planted the bomb. We're all better off."

Parting the Waters dealt with Martin Luther King and the civil rights movement from 1954 to 1963, part of an era Branch calls "the King years." In *Pillar of Fire* the time frame is much shorter, extending only from January of 1963 to the later part of 1965. Short though the time span is, these were years packed with great events that were to change the course of history. Branch seems determined to reconstruct a day-by-day record of absolutely everything that took place. This makes for a very long book that is not always easy reading. Trying to include everything means including a good deal that is comparatively dull or trivial. Trying to give an utterly fair, deadpan account of events sometimes produces sentences so confusing that Branch's editor seems to have been yawning when they slipped by.

Its defects, however, cannot diminish the grandeur of this book. I think of H. L. Mencken's judgment on Theodore Dreiser. Like Dreiser's, Branch's writing sometimes seems so plain and plodding that you wonder how he could have had a moment's pleasure in the act of creation, but, also as with Dreiser, the final, cumulative effect is overpowering. The sheer volume of fascinating stories accounts for this success.

We learn a great deal about the Black Muslims, their adulterous leader, Elijah Muhammad, and the murder of Malcolm X. The Vietnam War, soon to be a serious impediment to the civil rights movement, begins to develop. The war on poverty is launched. A landmark Supreme Court ruling on press freedom is issued. Harlem's playboy congressman, Adam Clayton Powell, loses a libel suit. We spend a depressing amount of time watching J. Edgar Hoover's half-demented struggle to preserve a dying past. President Kennedy is murdered and succeeded by the human hurricane that was Lyndon Johnson before Vietnam ruined him.

Branch is trying to write modern American history on an epic scale. It is not merely the story of Martin Luther King and the civil rights movement that he wants to tell. He is aiming for a big score: a full-length portrait of the United States during a crucial moment in its existence. His preface says the focus of his story is not Martin Luther King, but "the King years." In one of his rare lapses into meaningless pop jargon, Branch says he sees King's life as a "metaphor"—"the best and most important metaphor for American history in the watershed postwar years."

But what about those biblical titles? Is it America that God is leading out of captivity with his pillar of fire? Surely not. What grips us in *Pillar of Fire* is the melodrama of the civil rights movement, the bravery of the people who made it, the cruelty of the people who hated it, and in the end the nobility of Martin Luther King, who always knew he might be murdered at any moment, and always expected to be, and yet persisted.

Tales of heroism and villainy abound. There is the twenty-seven-year-old New Yorker Bob Moses running a one-man voter-registration drive in McComb, Mississippi.

> For trying to escort would-be voters to register, he had been arrested more than once, pummeled by a courthouse mob, and beaten severely near a town square in open daylight by a cousin of the Amite County sheriff. Still bleeding, he walked into the courthouse to file criminal charges, then testified against the cousin, and, until the local prosecutor advised him to flee for his life before a jury brought in the customary verdict of acquittal, continued doggedly to behave as though he possessed the natural rights of a white person. This presumption shocked Mississippi people more than the blood and terror.

There are the benighted sheriffs and police chiefs—Eugene T. "Bull" Connor of Birmingham, Jim Clark of Selma, Lawrence Rainey of Neshoba County, Mississippi—faithfully supporting the Hollywood image of the South as a land of Gothic horrors. Under their management, dogs are set upon demonstrators, high-pressure fire hoses turned against children, unarmed people punched and clubbed and kicked, houses dynamited, skulls fractured, churches burned, murders committed.

We visit Mississippi's infamous Parchman Penitentiary to which thirteen workers in a voter-registration campaign have been sentenced after the town of Greenwood loses its patience with them:

> Normally sullen guards greeted them expressly as recalcitrants to be broken, saying, "You're going to pay me." Shorn of hair from head to foot, every patch of stubble slathered in bluish delousing grease, they were marked apart from other inmates—the thirteen males crammed into cell number seven of the death

house built around Mississippi's gas chamber, with seven sleeping on the floor and one on the toilet. From there, guards shuffled them in more or less random punishment between isolation cells and the sweatbox, six feet square without lights or windows, vented only by a crack under the door.

...The punishment [for singing freedom songs to keep up their spirits] came to be hanging in handcuffs from a horizontal bar of his cell door. A guard informally sentenced Douglas Mac-Arthur Cotton to stretch beneath the handcuffs for forty-eight hours but took pity on him after three. Willy Carnell hung sleepless for a full thirty hours. Watkins and others lost track of how long they hung, but all of them, still singing or not, eventually gave way to helplessness and let their wastes fall down their prison-issue trouser legs.

2.

Long before King, everybody had known that America had a serious race problem, but there never seemed to be a convenient time for dealing with it. So much other serious business was always calling for immediate attention. Presidents especially were cruelly harried by other matters. The cold war, for instance. Taking on the race problem would have been highly inconvenient when survival of the free world was at stake. There were the newly warlike Chinese. You couldn't put Chairman Mao on the back burner, could you? He had the atom bomb. And what about the infestation of Communist conspirators working to destroy American democracy from within? Here was a truly dangerous domestic problem, and it consumed most of the political energy available for domestic problem-solving. Always, of course, another election lurked just over the horizon. What could be more inconvenient than taking on the race problem at election time? It was especially inconvenient for a Democratic president—John Kennedy, for example—who needed that solid bloc of Southern segregationist votes to keep him in the White House.

In the 1950s, stirrings on the race front began to disturb the White House. In 1954 the Supreme Court shocked the nation by declaring unanimously, in *Brown* v. *Board of Education*, that school segregation was unconstitutional. President Eisenhower was not happy about it. He hewed to the old saw about the uselessness of trying to change hearts and minds by passing laws. The architect of the *Brown* decision was Chief Justice Earl Warren, an Eisenhower appointee. Later Eisenhower said the Warren appointment was one of his biggest mistakes.

After its decision, the Court itself seemed dazed by what it had done and issued a mystifying order stating only that desegregation should proceed "with all deliberate speed." This was widely translated to mean, "No need for anybody to hurry."

In 1955 Washington was disturbed again when Rosa Parks ignited the Montgomery bus boycott by refusing to give up her seat to a white man. When Governor Orval Faubus of Arkansas ordered his National Guard to stop the desegregation of a Little Rock high school, Eisenhower had to send the army to Little Rock to enforce the law, but he hated having to do it.

It was during President Kennedy's term that the "freedom rides" occurred, the student sit-ins, the black boycotts, the nonviolent demonstrations in Albany, Georgia, and the white rioting incited by James Meredith's admission to the University of Mississippi. Neither the President nor his brother Robert, his attorney general, had spent much time pondering the politics of race. As members of a wealthy and sheltered white elite, they had little sense of the black experience or of middle-class white passions either. Race was not a thing they had expected to deal with when Jack was stumping the country pledging to "get this country moving again." They were absorbed by the Soviet threat to America; they saw the race problem primarily as a threat to Jack's reelection. The Kennedys' search for wiggle room between the South's racist white Democrats and the black disturbers of the status quo brought King to despair in 1963.

> After nearly three years, his relationship with President Kennedy had run out of room. Although the movement needed federal intervention more than ever, realism told King he could not pressure President Kennedy an inch further. Brooding, he took the young Justice Department lawyer Thelton Henderson privately aside [during a strategy conference]. "I'm concerned about having you in my meetings.... I'm worried that the Kennedys only want to know in advance if we're going to do something," he told Henderson. "Then they act to stop us. But they don't act when the whites do something. They just let us take another beating."

In his uneasiness about race, John Kennedy was not much different from most Americans of his generation. They had come of age in a time when *Gone With the Wind* was America's favorite movie and J. Edgar Hoover an American hero. The movie romanticized a slave society destroyed by brutal invaders, outside agitators, and dangerous black brutes. Hoover had been fighting for years to prevent a similar catastrophe from ever striking America again. In the 1930s he had saved us from John Dillinger and crime; in the 1940s, from Nazi spies. By the 1950s he was going after Communist conspirators and their dupes. Now he concentrated on blacks who were demanding equal justice under law.

By the 1960s all Washington took it for granted that, besides keeping an eye on the Reds, Hoover had everyone of any consequence under FBI surveillance. He certainly had a dossier on John Kennedy, and, as we now know, Kennedy was a rich subject for dossier compilers. Kennedy surely knew it, too. The day after the 1960 election, Kennedy made his very first presidential announcement: he had decided to reappoint Hoover as FBI director and Allen Dulles as head of the CIA.

Branch sees Kennedy as a cold warrior to whom civil rights became a distracting nuisance, as well as a political irritation. The question whether a Democratic president could "reduce the historic estrangement of Negroes" without losing his Southern white base "remained secondary to the national passions of the Cold War."

> Kennedy had won his office as a modern champion against Cold War enemies, pledging to redress a "missile gap" created by Republican laxity in the face of ominous Soviet advances.... President Eisenhower remarked that it was militarily "fantastic," "crazy," and "unconscionable" for the United States to have built some five thousand weapons averaging a hundred times the power of the Hiroshima bomb, be cranking out two more thermonuclear bombs every calendar day, and still push for more. Yet the respected commander of D-Day resigned himself as "only one person," helpless against the tide of arms.
>
> At his first press briefing as President Kennedy's incoming Secretary of Defense, Robert McNamara had disclosed that the celebrated missile gap did not exist after all. He retracted the statement under sharp public attack, and privately offered Kennedy his resignation. Remarkably, McNamara survived to swiftly remove Eisenhower's internal brakes on the development of strategic weapons.

The arms race roared ahead.

Lyndon Johnson was a different case. A harsh Texas upbringing had opened his eyes to injustices suffered by Mexicans. As Senate Democratic leader itching to be president, he had gone along with the Senate's powerful Southern committee chairmen, and it galled him that this political necessity had made it impossible for him ever to be nominated for the presidency. Now Johnson, thrust into the presidency, could at last show the world where he stood on race. He immediately made it clear that the full strength of the federal government would be placed behind the civil rights movement. For years American society had urged blacks to be patient, assuring them that equal rights would come later. With Johnson, the national policy abruptly changed from "later" to "now."

In 1964 he forced enactment of the first effective civil rights bill since Reconstruction. In 1965 came the Voting Rights Act, which was to change everything and, eventually, transform once rabidly segregationist politicians into seekers of black votes.

Even Johnson's most passionate liberal enemies were forced to ponder the possibility that, on the race issue at least, he was one of them. The surest evidence lies in a recorded private conversation with Senator Richard B. Russell, leader of the Senate's Southern bloc. A master of Senate procedure and politics, Russell had taught the young Johnson the arts that made him Senate majority leader very early in his career. They had never been personally closer than during Johnson's time in the White House. They talked daily about everything. Johnson spoke of it as a father–son relationship. On civil rights, however, Johnson was leaving the family, and he didn't hesitate to speak plainly. He and Russell had canvassed the hopelessness of his situation in Vietnam—Russell was chairman of the Senate Armed Services Committee—then turned to Johnson's civil rights bill.

"I'm not going to cavil and I'm not going to compromise," he told Russell. "I'm going to pass it just as it is, Dick, and if you get in my way I'm going to run you down. I just want you to know that because I care about you."

Russell replied: "Mr. President, you may be right. But if you do run over me, it will not only cost you the South, it will cost you the election."

Johnson was taking the risk despite knowing that the Democratic Party would pay a heavy price. Branch quotes him talking to his staff after signing the civil rights bill: "I think we just gave the South to the Republicans."

> Bill Moyers recalled Johnson saying that he had delivered the South to the Republicans "for your lifetime and for mine." ...In their direst visions, after the Goldwater convention followed hard upon the civil rights bill, neither established experts nor shell-shocked Negro Republicans anticipated a wholesale switch of party identification down to the roots of congressional and local offices.

This, of course, describes the American political scene today. The old solid Democratic South is now solidly Republican. For a brief moment under Johnson, the race problem had not been treated as an inconvenience, and the political consequences were shattering. Then Johnson began his descent into the bottomless pit of Vietnam, and everything began to fall apart. Martin Luther King had reservations about Vietnam. Johnson was displeased. King's reservations turned into outright opposition. Johnson was furious.

Pillar of Fire ends in 1965, before the break became irreparable, but *The Last Crusade*, by Gerald D. McKnight, takes King's story to the end with the Memphis murder in 1968.[2] McKnight is interested mainly in the Poor People's Campaign, which originated in 1967. By then King had lost faith in the existing political system. There had been a summer of rioting in Northern cities. It was now obvious that the black situation in the urban North was as desperate, in its own way, as it had been in the rural South. Bloody race violence in Detroit

---

2. *The Last Crusade: Martin Luther King, Jr., the* FBI, *and the Poor People's Campaign* (Westview, 1997).

and Newark left King despondent, saying, "There were dark days before, but this is the darkest."

"For King," McKnight says,

> Vietnam-era America was in the throes of a profound moral and political crisis. Its credibility abroad was crumbling, its cities were convulsed by rioting, and its values were corrupted by materialism. The national leadership, especially Congress, responded with trivial and half-hearted measures and searched for scapegoats while stolidly resisting real solutions.

He now saw race, war, and poverty as evils inextricably bound and decided that all three must be tackled as one. He angered Johnson by denouncing the Vietnam War. He outraged the Congress and scared many a Washington dweller with plans for a Poor People's Campaign to bring the lower-income masses to Washington. Comfortable people tend to be scared and angered when confronted by large-scale display of the economy's bottom-feeders. It reminds us of what comfortable people would rather forget: that it's ugly, mean, and dangerous down there.

In the jargon of the Sixties, King had been "radicalized." To many in that dismal age, "radicalized" people were hellbent on overthrowing the government and destroying "the American way of life." And so, in a way, King seemed finally to have made the paranoidal Hoover a prophet. He was now that dangerous character Hoover had visualized long ago after learning that one of King's associates had been a Communist. Near the end of his life, King had become a revolutionary.

3.

And so we come to J. Edgar Hoover. There is an immense literature about his single-minded determination to destroy King. David J. Garrow did the first heavy lifting on this subject with *The FBI and Martin Luther King* in 1981.[3] Branch cites it extensively and adds some new data of his own but, unlike Garrow, makes no attempt to explain the forces that drove Hoover. Analysis and interpretation are not Branch's style. He is a show-don't-tell historian, content to assemble mountains of facts, then let the reader make of them what he will. One misses an analysis of Hoover. What a wonderful time Macaulay would have had with this terrifying old tyrant whose eyes and ears were everywhere.

Branch is no Macaulay, and obviously doesn't wish to be. He is content to present Hoover in bits and pieces. Was he a racist? Branch has an oral history fragment with Bobby Kennedy saying Hoover believed the brains of black people were twenty percent smaller than whites'. There is the moment, after hearing tapes of King's amatory evening in the Willard Hotel, when Hoover gloats, "This will destroy the burrhead." To speed up King's destruction, he has FBI well-poisoners concoct an anonymous letter, mail it to King with the tape, and urge him to kill himself.

Hoover prowls Branch's book like an ogre. Now he is letting President Kennedy know that his extramarital sex life is an open book to the FBI. Now he is exploiting President Johnson's feud with Bobby Kennedy to destroy the attorney general's power. His aide, Cartha D. DeLoach, presents him with a document describing King as "a vicious liar" who uses "deceit, lies and treachery as propaganda to further his own causes," and Hoover writes, "I concur."

Hoover learns that one Ellen Rometsch from Communist East Germany is one of John Kennedy's sex partners and alerts Bobby, who has her spirited out of the country. Then Bobby must go to Hoover, asking him to persuade congressmen not to leak the story. Bobby assumes that Hoover has ways of making congressmen not talk. They don't.

---

3. Norton, 1981.

Hoover is also watching the CIA. He notifies the White House that the agency has sought the cooperation of three Mafia godfathers in murdering Fidel Castro. One of them, he reveals, is Sam Giancana, and Giancana's mistress, Hoover lets the White House know, has been sharing the President's bed. Hoover suggests the President end the affair.

Here Branch steps out of character briefly to pass a judgment and allow himself a small sigh of amazement:

> This was sordid business—gangster-spy assassination plots, molls and Mata Haris in the President's bed, blackmail between branches of government—all beyond the era's capacity for cynical imagination.

Garrow's book attempts to explain Hoover in cultural terms, suggesting that he was not an idiosyncratic wild man but a reasonable expression of one important part of American society:

> ... The essence of the Bureau's social role has been not to attack critics, Communists, blacks, or leftists per se, but to repress all perceived threats to the dominant, status-quo-oriented political culture.... The Bureau was not a deviant institution in American society, but actually a most representative and faithful one.... The enemies chosen by the F.B.I. were the same targets that much of American society would have selected as its own foes. American popular thought long has had strong themes of nativism, xenophobia, and ethnocentrism. These very same qualities were writ large in the F.B.I.

In "the King years" many Americans were angry and fearful about longhaired youth, rock music, campus rebellions, free-speech agitators, rising drug use, the casual new sexual code, and opposition to the Vietnam War. All this looked to many like an assault on America itself, an effort to destroy a successful, orderly society symbolized by short haircuts, the Ozzie-and-Harriet family, the Glenn Miller Band, respect for professors and presidents, and readiness to say, "My country, right or wrong!" The civil rights movement, of course, was part of this assault on the old order. Millions who liked things the way they used to be might well have thought Hoover was doing the Lord's work.

Branch finds that while King was Hoover's prime black target, Malcolm X and the Honorable Elijah Muhammad's Nation of Islam were also under surveillance. Branch deals extensively with the split between Malcolm and Elijah Muhammad, even devoting his opening chapter to a bloody battle between Muslims and police at a temple in South-Central Los Angeles. Malcolm's open declarations of hostility toward white America suggest an era of violence that might have been, were it not for convictions of Southern blacks that they could succeed only by following Gandhi's philosophy of nonviolence. This required them to take the white man's clubbing without striking back. Malcolm had no patience with people willing to submit to brutality.

Branch's Malcolm is an angry man of principle becoming seriously devoted to the Islamic faith and, as he does, becoming disgusted with the corruption surrounding Elijah Muhammad. He allows, however, for the possibility that Malcolm may also have been trying to overthrow the old man and take over. Branch tells us very little about the religious aspect of the Nation and nothing at all about its origins. Elijah Muhammad, born Elijah Poole in rural Georgia, was its absolute master when Malcolm appeared. It had been founded in the 1930s by one Wallace D. Fard. Elijah Poole, "humiliated into alcoholism by relief lines," was one of Fard's most zealous followers. There seems to have been a violent struggle for the succession during which Poole sometimes had to hide out from murderous competitors.

Branch introduces Elijah after the shoot-out with the Los Angeles police at the Muslim temple. Malcolm had persuaded two high-powered lawyers of the black bourgeoisie to defend the Muslims charged with assaulting the police. They were astonished when they met the Nation's leader. They found

> a wizened, wheezy old man of sixty-four years—to them a field hand in a fez, plainly ignorant and inarticulate as he mumbled thanks for helping "my mens." Utterly astonished that Muhammad held any authority over someone of Malcolm X's polished commitment, the lawyers avoided each other's eyes to keep from laughing impolitely at the attendants who constantly uttered obeisance to the "Holy Apostle."

One wants to know more about Wallace Fard. Branch says only that he was a "mysterious silk dealer" who "disappeared." Transformed into Elijah Muhammad, Poole became tyrannical; as he aged, the Nation was threatened by various crises. His oldest son, Elijah Jr., saw it being torn by "threats, thefts, scandals, plots, betrayals, and rampant fears that Malcolm X might usurp the entire structure if the sickly old man died soon."

Malcolm learned that Elijah had sired illegitimate children by two of his former secretaries, who were demanding recognition and support. Malcolm cultivated Wallace Muhammad, Elijah's seventh child, who was spiritually committed to the religious principles of Islam and repelled by what was happening in the Nation. "The corrupt hypocrites high in the organization," he said, "throw people out for smoking a cigarette while they themselves were drinking champagne and going to orgies."

> Wallace confessed that several of his own relatives prospered off the Nation without knowing the first thing about Islam.

His stories about power struggles over jewelry and real estate touched a nerve, and the two men [Wallace and Malcolm] fell into collusion.

Malcolm made a life-threatening move when he tried to publicize Elijah Muhammad's illicit sexual relationships, and was finally murdered for it. Three trained killers gunned him down as he spoke to a New York audience. Elijah Muhammad had apparently declared a *fatwa* against him before then, for Branch tells of Malcolm being pursued with gunfire in wild car chases through the streets.

Malcolm had hoped to stir up public anger about Muhammad's abuse of Islamic principle. Publicity might produce enough anger to turn the old man out, but nobody who mattered much was bothering to listen, except J. Edgar Hoover. He had known about the bastard children three years before Malcolm and had also tried, without success, to draw public attention to them.

Generating public attention had become the key to victory in political struggles, and no one knew it better than King. Branch suggests that King's decision to attack segregation in Birmingham was based on a calculation that it was the place most likely to provide him with the national attention the movement desperately needed. If so, television can claim to have played a heroic role in the movement.

By 1963 television was radically changing American culture. Political success now required television exposure. The public tended to pay attention to what television paid attention to. The way to stir up public interest was to interest television, and the way to interest television was to exploit its need for brief dramas that could be shown in pictures with high emotional impact. Television trafficked in feelings. Its interviewers were constantly asking, "How does it feel?" "How do you feel?" "What does (or did) it feel like?" Its nature was to stir audience emotions—the quicker, the better. Time for television was big money. It wanted brief moments dramatic enough to produce public emotions.

Before 1963 the people comprising the civil rights movement had enjoyed only occasional successes at capturing national attention. In Albany, Georgia, a shrewd sheriff had cleverly avoided situations conducive to the kind of violence that makes dramatic television. The Albany campaign had begun late in 1961, dragged unsuccessfully into 1962, and ran out of gas. By late 1962 King seemed to have failed in the attempt to arouse enough public passion to force the Kennedys to intervene. Then, late that winter, he decided to take the struggle to Birmingham. Here was a crossing of the Rubicon.

The hundredth anniversary of the Emancipation Proclamation came and went with no gesture of support from Kennedy. King met with his ten closest associates and told them, Branch writes, that "there was no easy button to push, no executive alliance to be made."

> All the dignified routes had been closed off. The only paths he saw led either to retreat or forward over the cliff, and, haunted by fear that the integrationist mandate of the Supreme Court's 1954 *Brown* decision and the energy of the Kennedy years would soon dissipate, King disclosed his resolve to take a calculated leap...a staged, nonviolent assault on Birmingham, the symbolic bastion of segregation—a city that combined the plantation attitudes of the surrounding Alabama counties with the bare-knuckled politics of its steel-mill economy, personified in both aspects by the local police commissioner, Eugene T. "Bull" Connor.
>
> Instead of avoiding risks, or grumbling about the moral obtuseness in the press, King's forces would embrace the public drama of a showdown between King and Bull Connor.

Connor rewarded him with a confrontation that was irresistible to television. Birmingham, Connor, snarling police dogs, jailed children, a jailed King—suddenly the civil rights movement was a major item on the national agenda. "Bull" Connor's dumbness became a blessing for the movement.

Glenn T. Eskew's *But for Birmingham* differs about Birmingham.[4] His is a valuable academic study of Birmingham society, economics, and politics, and though written in clotted thesis prose, provides a more complex view of the city in 1963 than we are accustomed to. He points out that white Birmingham was not a unified citadel of bigotry, but that a substantial part of its white population, including important business interests, wanted a moderate settlement. Among these elements, "Bull" Connor was disliked if not detested.

Eskew has an especially good portrait of Connor, including the hilarious story of his being impeached after a Birmingham detective, accompanied by a news photographer, caught him in a hotel room with his secretary. We learn that, like Ronald Reagan, Connor had a youthful career broadcasting baseball games on the basis of a few skimpy facts about balls and strikes telegraphed into a radio studio.

Eskew also has a nice reconstruction of the critical moment when King in Birmingham decides to defy the court's injunction against marching, though he knows it will expose him to whatever risk a hated black agitator might face in the Birmingham jail.

> If he declined to march, he would forever be a failure. As he later observed, "What would be the verdict of the country about a man who had encouraged hundreds of people to make a stunning sacrifice and then excused himself?" Feeling the "deepest quiet" he had ever experienced, King looked out at the expressions of those gathered in the motel suite and came "face to face with himself." He felt "alone in that crowded room." In despair, King broke away to pray for an answer. As he "stood in the

4. *But for Birmingham: The Local and National Movements in the Civil Rights Struggle* (University of North Carolina Press, 1997).

center of the floor" in the adjoining chamber, he recalled, "I think I was standing also in the center of all that my life had brought me to be." ... He changed into a new pair of dungarees and stepped back into the suite, announcing, "The path is clear to me. I've got to march."

King's life may or may not be Branch's "important metaphor" for American history since the end of World War II. Surely, however, he was the bravest of those who walked those gaudy years and probably the best.

Chapter 6

WHERE HAS JOE GONE?

1.

JOE DIMAGGIO PLAYED baseball for the New York Yankees for thirteen years, then spent the rest of his life playing Joe DiMaggio. It is doubtful that he enjoyed either career very much, or that he enjoyed anything at all very deeply, although Richard Ben Cramer's *Joe DiMaggio: The Hero's Life* suggests that he took a miser's delight in accumulating money.[1] Even this pleasure was often spoiled by suspicions that friends and relatives were raking in money that should have been his. Joylessness seems to have been his natural habitat, distrust his natural instinct, and loneliness his inevitable destiny. He had no enduring friendships, but he had a hundred "pals," each of whom, like a typical specimen described by Cramer, "had blisters on his lips from kissing the ground Joe walked on." He was married twice, both times to blond actresses, both of whom divorced him. By the first he had a son to whom he was an indifferent, mostly absent father. The son outlived him by only six months, then died of an overdose of heroin and crack cocaine.

To escape California taxes, DiMaggio in old age moved from his native San Francisco to Hollywood, Florida, where, though now in

---

1. Simon and Schuster, 2000.

his eighties, he still took in huge sums of money by selling autographed memorabilia to collectors. When he was eighty-three years old and terribly sick, the yearning for one last big payday took him on a four-day trip to Chicago and New York, where George Steinbrenner laid on a Joe DiMaggio Day at Yankee Stadium and presented him with replicas of his nine World Series rings. He died five months later, totally dependent on the Florida lawyer who managed his business, his estate, his hospital care, and his manner of departure from this world.

Thus Cramer's melancholy portrait of a very inferior hero. Why does it seem so sad, even shocking? That a celebrated athlete may also be a mass of human frailties is common knowledge now to all but the most gullible fan. Nowadays we are all onto the inglorious reality of the athlete's life. The sports pages, which once were filled with mythical gods and enchanted boys of summer at play in the Land of Let's Pretend, are now given over to humdrum financial and medical news. Greed and pulled hamstrings are the modern sportswriter's daily subject matter. All but the dimmest fan now know that "sport" is an ironic euphemism for a ruthless multibillion-dollar branch of the entertainment industry and that the game too often played by its CEOs is extortion. ("Either this town pays to build me a new place of business, or I move the team to a town that will.")

Everybody knows all this, knows too about the greedy insolence and nasty characters of too many athletes, but Joe DiMaggio was different, wasn't he? Sure he had been a superb ballplayer, but it was his elegant character that made him different from all other ballplayers. It was what made him uniquely fit to be exalted. People constantly said that DiMaggio had "class," had "dignity," was a man of "elegance." As a ballplayer of course DiMaggio was "great," but baseball had "greats" galore. Ted Williams and Willie Mays were "great." Ty Cobb, half mad and dangerously violent, was "great." But DiMaggio was something more majestic than "great." DiMaggio was special. Men would "display awe at his presence, joy at his godlike glory," writes Cramer.

"... He had been touched ... as if the Hand of God had reached down and made this man great—uncommon, unlike them...."

Cramer tells us: Believe that and you'll believe anything. The burden of his message is that we have been gulled, for the DiMaggio to whom a nation turned its mournful eyes with veneration at his death in 1999 was a hollow construction of the publicity industry. Alas for another failed god. Books like this are among the penalties that celebrities must endure for growing old. Heroes age best by dying young. Would Achilles be admired today if Apollo and Paris had not killed him in his youth? Imagine an eighty-five-year-old Achilles who might have been: a stooped codger waving from a replica Trojan Horse as he enters Agamemnon Stadium for Old-Timers Day. Instead of Homer to lionize him for the ages, he would surely have ended up in the merciless clasp of an Attic myth-busting precursor of Richard Ben Cramer.

Cramer is out to destroy an edifice that took our national engines of ballyhoo, bushwah, and baloney half a century to create. The "hero machine," as he calls it, is as much Cramer's subject as DiMaggio's banal frailties. If there is a villain here it is "the hero machine," and DiMaggio seems most sympathetic when Cramer casts him as its victim. Trying to explain his marriage to Marilyn Monroe, Cramer does some gaudy theorizing about the terrors ordinary people must feel after being inflated by "the hero machine":

> Joe and Marilyn had one big thing in common.... Both were living inside the vast personages that the hero machine had created for them. And inside those personages—those enormous idols for the nation—these two, Marilyn and Joe, were only small and struggling, fearful to be seen. And alone—always. They were like kids, left in a giant house, and they must not be discovered. Or it would all come crashing down. In their loneliness, they might have been brother and sister.
>
> Joe's insistence made them husband and wife.

Cramer never offers a description of his "hero machine," but its basic structure is obvious. There is the natural alliance between team operators and sportswriters to stimulate business for both. A band of heroes will attract more readers and bigger box office than a group of ordinary men in baseball suits. When DiMaggio surfaced in the 1930s, sportswriting was still enjoying a remarkably creative period. It attracted journalism's finest writers while also producing a great deal of terrible prose by bush-league Hemingways dying to show off in print. Top-drawer or hack, the sportswriter was licensed to let his creative impulse romp free.

One technique was to imbue their sweaty subject matter with legend and myth. As a sportswriter you could turn the most bone-headed bozo into Hercules. Golden Ages sprang out of battered typewriters, huge crowds were constantly "electrified," and many an earth-bestriding giant filled sports pages like a colossus. What bliss it must have been to write sports then. You could give humanity a miracle, as some typewriter artist did by creating "the miracle of Coogan's Bluff." (Translation: Player hits home run at Polo Grounds; Giants win pennant. It was no mere home run, admittedly, but "the shot heard round the world.") You could turn a pudgy slum kid from Baltimore into "the Sultan of Swat" and endow him with the awesome power to afflict the Boston Red Sox with "the curse of the Bambino." Grantland Rice could watch a football game and, in the four young men of the Notre Dame backfield, see the Four Horsemen of the Apocalypse—Famine, Pestilence, Destruction, and Death—forming "the crest of the South Bend cyclone."

The hero's buildup for DiMaggio differed from the normal by continuing long after he left baseball. His name began to figure in worlds alien to baseball. Oscar Hammerstein, in a lyric for the Broadway hit *South Pacific*, wrote of a woman whose skin was "tender as DiMaggio's glove." Ernest Hemingway, writing *The Old Man and the Sea*, had his old Cuban fisherman indulge in some suspiciously

Hemingwayesque musings about "the great DiMaggio." Tin Pan Alley produced a tune about "Joltin' Joe DiMaggio." In 1975, a quarter-century after his retirement, a movie version of Raymond Chandler's *Farewell My Lovely* had Philip Marlowe checking the newspapers day after day to see if DiMaggio had hit.

In 1967 Paul Simon's memorable song to "Mrs. Robinson," the corrupt adulterous seducer of Dustin Hoffman in *The Graduate*, celebrated a new kind of DiMaggio heroism for a new generation without memory of his baseball triumphs. Simon's lyric, asking "Where have you gone, Joe DiMaggio?," became a lament for the fancied loss of an innocent America. Simon's "nation" that turned "its lonely eyes" to DiMaggio seemed to be the postwar baby boomers who were already making life hell for parents—like corrupt middle-age Mrs. Robinson. Making DiMaggio represent an innocent America, more pure than adulterous Mrs. Robinson's, was silly of course, and not just because of his busy sex life. The most famous line in *The Graduate* was a single word: "Plastics." That was where a young man ought to look for success, Dustin Hoffman was advised. Audiences laughed with cynical recognition: "Plastics." It spoke so trenchantly of an America aspiring to a shabby materialism. But DiMaggio was an absurd hero for antimaterialists. As Cramer illustrates, DiMaggio would have been overjoyed to get in on the ground floor to make a killing in plastics.

Cramer has two other main themes: DiMaggio's obsession with money and the sadness of beautiful youth outliving its time. The two are intertwined in his opening pages. We first see DiMaggio only a few months from death. He is a tottering, sick old man with a pacemaker and a cancerous lung, appearing at Yankee Stadium on one last moneymaking expedition. DiMaggio "seemed a sad figure," Cramer writes. "It wasn't just the effects of age—the way he'd shrunk—that bent old man who took his rings behind home plate and tottered off the field.... More to the point, it was his cloak of myth that had shrunk. The lies around him were growing cheap."

One lie involved George Steinbrenner's gift of the replicas of the allegedly stolen rings on that last Joe DiMaggio Day. DiMaggio "didn't lose those rings to theft," Cramer asserts. "More likely he traded them for free lodging, food, transportation, services of every kind." That day was not about rings, but about "money, mostly money, as it mostly was with Joe."

Here we immediately confront a serious problem with Cramer as a historian. This is a book without a single footnote. With no attribution whatever, stories scandalous, shocking, and delightful are presented as gospel. How does Cramer know those rings weren't stolen? We are expected to trust him. His credentials are good. He has a Pulitzer Prize for journalism. *What It Takes*, his book on the men who ran for president in 1988, is one of the best of its sort ever written. Still, some of his juiciest DiMaggio stories rely entirely on Cramer's say-so with no corroborating witness. Respectable though Cramer is at his trade, this is apt to leave the finicky reader uneasy.

Part of Cramer's problem is DiMaggio's astonishing success in keeping his real life—as opposed to his fictional hero life—to himself. All his life he refused to talk to biographers, including Cramer, and any associate or pal who talked was exiled from the DiMaggio aura. With DiMaggio refusing to talk and everybody else afraid to talk, it has never been easy to find people willing to go public with gee-whiz tales about him.

Take Cramer's story about the $600,000 in cash which DiMaggio carried out of his San Francisco house in a plastic garbage bag the evening of the earthquake of 1989. Some story! Joe rushing home to find his neighborhood devastated, police not letting anybody into their houses but making an exception for Joe of course, and Joe going in, then coming out with garbage bag in hand and lugging it off to the Presidio Club where he spends the night. Where did that money come from? How long had it been there? Did the IRS know about it? Cramer doesn't tell us, and what is more galling, he gives no clue to how he could have known there was $600,000 in that bag.

We are also asked to trust Cramer's say-so about gangsters routinely putting money in a DiMaggio account at the Bowery Bank. And what of the story that forty years ago the gangster Abner ("Longy") Zwillman gave DiMaggio "boxes" of his ill-gotten money for safekeeping and that Joe was still keeping them safe when Longy's irritated colleagues produced his suicide by hanging Longy from a chandelier? Cramer offers no clue to the provenance of this story, though he leaves us to understand it was Longy's money that Joe carried off in the garbage bag and that Joe had kept it for the forty years after Longy's death. Whether out of reverence for the dead or ignorance about money laundering, we can only guess.

Cramer's prose is freewheeling and journalistic, with heavy use of the vernacular and occasional satirical mockery of old-fashioned breezy sports-page diction. (Runs are "plated," not "scored." Joe's testy refusals to pose for photographers are "vehemed," not "snarled.") It is a style better suited to fiction than to history. And why not? If the subject is baseball, Elmore Leonard is probably preferable to Arnold Toynbee.

2.

When DiMaggio joined the Yankees at age twenty-one he was coming to publicity heaven: New York City, home office of worldwide ballyhoo. It was a city with a prodigious appetite for stars of all varieties. New York did not put up with ordinary actors, ordinary boxers, ordinary singers, musicians, writers, ballplayers, geniuses, gangsters, saloonkeepers, or sturgeon slicers. Ordinariness was small-town. New York fed on a steady diet of stars, preferably stars of the first magnitude. In a thin season those not of the first magnitude could be made to glow with New York's inexhaustible supply of glory-enhancing publicity gas.

DiMaggio didn't need enhancing. He was a press agent's dream, a man-child so innocent that he didn't even know what a "quote" was when the sportswriters asked him for one. He thought it might be a soft drink. But he was not just unformed innocence waiting to have a persona shaped for him by the forces of blather and flapdoodle; he was an athlete of surpassing excellence, a natural, a mere kid so good at his work that sportswriters wouldn't have to overwork their adjectives to sell him to the fans. For Cramer's "hero machine," he was a dream come true. The innocence was part of what made him good copy. He seemed uneasy to the point of terror about social encounters. Cramer suggests this reflected his family's Sicilian background, which taught the wisdom of keeping your head down. Maybe, but DiMaggio had two other brothers, Dominic and Vince, who played professional baseball, and both were readily accessible to the public. Cramer suggests that Vince was even a joyful figure. Perhaps Joe was simply born uneasy. Whatever the case, his restrained, distant, occasionally surly manner made good material for writers.

In 1936, when DiMaggio showed up, the sports pages had a glut of stars acting at being just regular guys. Poor Joe Louis, possibly the best heavyweight ever, had to stand by patiently while racists praised him as "a credit to his race," thereby suggesting that African-Americans were a low-credit bunch while assuring the crowd that "the Brown Bomber" was just another regular guy, and not a brown menace. DiMaggio created a more interesting possibility for publicity artists. They could write about his aura of mystery and his dignity, and as the years passed these became clichés of DiMaggio literature.

It seems more likely that he came to New York as a shy, scared, insecure country boy might have come to some terrifying metropolis in a Ring Lardner tale about a hick ballplayer afraid he will be humiliated if the world discovers he doesn't know how to tip a cab driver or sign a bar check. Typically, Joe liked Superman comic books but was afraid to be seen buying one, so had somebody do it for him. Even as a sandlot ballplayer in San Francisco he had had a young man called "Shirts" DeMarco hanging around to do him services and deflect unwanted intrusions. With instant fame in New York, he quickly began attracting more sophisticated men as buffers between himself and the complicated world of New York celebrity. These men existed to do things for him: to accompany him to dinner, order for him, deflect worshipful nuisances, arrange an assignation with a woman who caught his eye, pay the bill, or make sure that the house was aware that bills were not to be rendered to Mister DiMaggio.

With a long procession of these human buffers, always working for the pleasure of being known as Joe's pals, DiMaggio enjoyed a fully serviced life. Until the day of his death there was scarcely a time when his needs and wants were not seen to by others. Cramer's tales of men who buffered for DiMaggio depict a kind of boy's-club life. A lot of it was lived at Toots Shor's restaurant where the guys gathered after the game—ballplayers, sportswriters, maybe some hoods but no big-timers when Joe was there since Frank Costello, the super capo, was protective of Joe's image. So was Toots. "Crumbums," as Toots called people who annoyed Joe, were shown the door. Wives were welcome as long as a husband didn't make a regular thing of it. The buffer was expected to be ready to drop everything at Joe's call and report for duty. Cramer paraphrases the *New York Times* sportswriter Louis Effrat at length about palship with Joe:

> Say, for example, the Clipper was at Shor's, when some broad would be brought to his table to meet the Great DiMaggio. Joe would modestly shake her hand—that was all . . . until he called for Lou. When Effrat got to Joe's corner, DiMaggio would murmur, "See that blond in the black dress? Take her to the late show at El Morocco. Tell the maitre d' you're at my table." Louis would race to a phone and call Brooklyn—eleven P.M. or midnight—

he'd wake his wife, Alice: "I'll be late. I'm going out with the Dago!" She knew he'd have to squire some girl around for Di-Maggio. But she didn't protest. She could hear the fever in his voice. Then, Lou would leave with the girl. ("Joe will be along to meet us, in a while...") Sure, there might be a columnist—photographers for sure—working the floor at El Morocco. But if anybody asked, it wasn't Joe had a date with the girl. No, Effrat had the date.

If DiMaggio saw women as consumer goods that were part of the young hero's entitlement, he took the old-fashioned masculine view of the two he married. To both Dorothy Arnold and Marilyn Monroe his behavior was protective and proprietary. Both wanted careers; Di-Maggio wanted housewives. Both bridled at the idea of waiting for Joe to come home from work so they could snuggle down watching television. DiMaggio hated the notion of other men thinking of his wives as he himself thought of other women. Jealousy enraged him when he saw Marilyn Monroe being marketed as sexual goods. She delighted in it. Divorce was inevitable; the marriage lasted only 286 days. DiMaggio grew old hating Hollywood and all its crowd (including its auxiliary Kennedy family), who, as he thought, had exploited, abused, and then destroyed his wife.

Cramer doesn't dwell long on the Marilyn Monroe story, probably because it has been told and retold and nothing new is left to tell. The comic-opera aspect of their marriage is expressed to perfection in a line he excavates from a book by Marilyn's half-sister. Abandoning DiMaggio's protection in San Francisco, Marilyn tells her sister she is going to Los Angeles as the guest of Frank Sinatra, "because I need some total privacy."

DiMaggio's obsession with money seems to date from childhood when he sold newspapers at streetcar stops. Each paper cost three cents, of which the newsboy kept a penny, but DiMaggio mastered the art of having so much trouble finding change that buyers who gave him a nickel would tell him to keep the other two cents.

In signing with the Yankees, he was dealing with major-league penny-pinchers. They offered $5,625 a year to start. (Today's offer for such a spectacular talent would probably approach $1 million.) A canny old baseball man who had befriended DiMaggio had a canny old acquaintance "who could squeeze a nickel till the buffalo on it was dead from lack of air." He was Ty Cobb. Cobb dictated DiMaggio's refusal to Yankee general manager Ed Barrow, famous for cheap pay, and Barrow countered by offering $6,500. Cobb "dictated to Joe an even more polite and implacable response." Barrow sent a third contract offering $8,500 and a note saying, "*This is the limit. Don't waste another three-cent stamp. Just sign it. And tell Cobb to stop writing me letters.*" (Cramer's italics.)

After his first two sensational seasons the Yankees taught him a profoundly embittering lesson about the market value of heroes. They offered $25,000 and DiMaggio said he wanted $40,000. The Yankees didn't bother to negotiate. They didn't have to. In those days players were the wholly owned property of their teams. This resulted from a bizarre court ruling that because baseball was "sport," not business, a team owner had exclusive rights to negotiate with team members "for the good of the game." DiMaggio could play for the Yankees' $25,000, or he could refuse, but he could not sell his services to another team. All he could do was "hold out" by staying at home on the chance that the Yankees might need him enough to sweeten their offer.

The Yankees had ways of making proud men bend. The machine that makes heroes can also unmake them. The word "greed" was spread among the fans. Twenty-five thousand was big money in a country that still thought $5,000 a year was a rich man's pay. Joe McCarthy, the team manager, turned against him. "The Yankees can get along without DiMaggio," he said. His surrender was inevitable. The

Yankees—why are they so often praised as the epitome of "class"?—couldn't resist rubbing it in.

Cramer describes the Yankee owner Jacob Ruppert making "a series of triumphal announcements": DiMaggio's contract would have "no bonus clauses, nothing extra. And Joe would not get a dime till he got in shape at his own expense: about a hundred fifty a day in lost wages. Meanwhile, if he wanted to travel with the club, he could pay his own train fare, hotel, and meals." Ruppert said, "I hope the young man has learned his lesson."

There was still more to learn: the fans began to boo. Cramer quotes DiMaggio saying, "Pretty soon I got the idea the only reason people come to the game at all is to boo DiMaggio. And the mail! You would have thought I'd kidnapped the Lindbergh baby, the way some of the letters read."

"Joe had learned lessons," writes Cramer,

> but not the ones Ruppert intended. He's learned that the fans could turn against him . . . [that] the writers were all in bed with the club—Joe was convinced of that—they'd turned the fans against him. . . . Now, Joe understood: they would never pay him what he was worth—not fairly, not willingly . . . and he couldn't make them pay. Now Joe knew, he was hired help. No one ever made hired help rich.

This angry, embittered man was only twenty-three years old.

In the old man the youthful rage became a neurotic obsession with money. He developed a "legendary disinclination to pay" for anything. His business was being Joe DiMaggio, and part of it consisted in obtaining necessary goods and services for free.

> . . . His was not a simple cheapness: it wasn't just paying that drove Joe nuts. It was even when he didn't pay, when he was

getting money, even when he was *getting millions*. That's when
he took it one step beyond...
  Who else would make money in the deal?
  How much?
  Why should those guys make a buck off my life?

Cramer doesn't say how much money DiMaggio had at his death,
though he refers vaguely to millions in earnings, largely from ventures
in the booming baseball memorabilia business. This involves selling
autographed pictures, cards, balls, and such to people who pay astonishing prices for it. It is eloquent testimony to the cheapness of the
baseball owners that the finest players of the DiMaggio era can now
earn more as geezers peddling gimcracks than they did when they
were golden lads bringing glory to the game.

That DiMaggio brought glory to baseball is indisputable. If he
played Joe DiMaggio very badly, he seems to have played baseball
majestically. Cramer suggests that he was born gifted with an instinct
for baseball. He apparently mastered the game without struggle and
played it with a graceful beauty that awed those who saw him.
Statistics, by which baseball fans measure quality, suggest he had few
equals as a hitter. He was an essential player for a team that played in
nine World Series and lost only one.

In 1941 he did something that had never been done before by getting a hit in fifty-six consecutive games. Sportswriters constantly
assure us that this is such an amazing feat that no player will ever
duplicate it. Maybe not, but don't bet the house on it. Baseball
authorities are constantly redesigning their game to keep up with
trends in the tastes of its fans. Recent manipulations have produced
so many home-run sluggers that the thrill of the old-fashioned
Homeric clout is gone. Money is as vital to the owners today as it
was when the Yankees were ready to crush DiMaggio's spirit rather
than offer him another $5,000. If it looks financially profitable to

have DiMaggio's record broken, well—Major League Baseball has ways of making the impossible happen.

In his youth baseball came so easily to DiMaggio that he seemed inhuman—a child, said a publicity artist, who had been created by God to play baseball as Mozart had been created to make music. It was not so easy to feel warmth for such a player as one felt for, say, the joyfully boyish Willie Mays or that lumpen reform-school rascal Babe Ruth. As DiMaggio aged, however, the game ceased being child's play, and his body began letting him down. For the first time he had to struggle as normal players had always had to struggle to be good at the game. "Joe has suddenly been taken old," someone wrote, and he became painfully human. The struggling required to be good was not enough of course; being DiMaggio, he had to struggle even harder in order to be better than anyone else.

Cramer is brutal in dismantling the image that the "hero machine" created during the sixty-two years of DiMaggio's public life. He has only praise, however, for the character of the DiMaggio who played baseball:

> He wanted to be, in any year, any town, on any day, any field—in every game, on every play, no matter who else was there—the best player in the park. He wanted to be the man in whose hands the fate of the game would rest. He expected to deliver that game, every game, to his team. He expected to dominate, not by doing something right, but by doing everything right.... He wanted to be perfect, not at something but everything.

Does this reveal DiMaggio as a man eager "to abide...as a god"? Cramer says it does, but one suspects he is groggy from too much immersion in "hero machine" malarkey. The DiMaggio his book portrays was almost always too frail, too pathetic, too human to aspire to divine eminence. He was a lonely, unhappy, empty man who could do one extraordinarily difficult thing better than almost anybody else in the world, and was proud of it, as he was entitled to be.

Chapter 7

THE EXILE

AMONG THOSE WHO came to his funeral were President Clinton and four former presidents: Gerald Ford, Jimmy Carter, Ronald Reagan, and George Bush. He had no doubt that he was superior to them all. Admittedly, Watergate—"that silly, silly thing"—had been a lapse, but in his opinion, when it came to presidential business that truly mattered, not one of those eminent mourners was in the same league with Richard Nixon.

Monica Crowley thinks so, too. The conviction has prompted her to issue two memoirs creating a portrait of Nixon, as the title of her second book, *Nixon in Winter*,[1] puts it, in the winter of his life. The burden of them is that he was a far more admirable figure than widely supposed, a president who got a dirty deal from powerful forces— "armies of enemies"—who hated him. Hers is not the Nixon of the Watergate tapes, but a genial, complicated, avuncular old fellow in whom most of the bile, not all but most, is spent.

She has nothing new to report on Watergate, but who has? The familiar defenses are mounted again. They all did it, Nixon was the victim of an unfair double standard, and so forth. For historians there is nothing of consequence, either, in what Nixon said to her about the

---

1. Random House, 1998.

Vietnam War, the Cambodian invasion, or the secretive foreign policy in which he connived with an equally manipulative Henry Kissinger.

What is irresistible, however, is the powerful sense she conveys of Nixon's personality when he was playing the endgame of his long struggle to come back from disgrace. This results from her use of extensive quotations. We often seem to be listening to yet another batch of Nixon tapes or, perhaps, tapes of another Nixon so different from the Watergate tapes that he seems to have undergone a character transformation. It is gossipy, outrageous, comical, fascinating, entertaining, delightful stuff.

To evaluate Crowley's Nixon, it helps to know something about Crowley herself. She worked for him for the last four years of his life, and her devotion clearly bordered on adoration. She was twenty-one when she started: Nixon was seventy-seven, old enough to have been her grandfather. She was born in 1968, the year he was elected president. Her first memory of him was of watching his televised announcement that he was resigning the presidency. She was then five years old.

He had been out of office some fifteen years when they first met. He had spent every one of those years laboring to rebuild a reputation shattered by Watergate. These labors included a tireless book-writing program. The books presented him as a sage elder statesman whose knowledge and experience of great events could be invaluable to the nation, if Washington would only bring him out of exile and heed his messages. Discussing a work-in-progress with Crowley, he told her, "I'm writing this book not because I need to do it for myself but because the country needs to hear this kind of realism from me." Years had passed with no one who counted listening to his realism.

Still, he went to the end without giving up. During Crowley's brief time with him, he traveled to Russia and China, no idle journeys for a man teetering at the edge of eighty. Comically, in Russia he infuriated Boris Yeltsin by meeting with Yeltsin's political opponents. Yeltsin reacted by cutting off Nixon's transportation and security privileges and canceling his appointments with government people. Afterward, at 5:00 AM in Moscow, Nixon phoned Crowley in America, telling her, "Yeltsin, of course, had had a few when he erupted at me. That's well-known."

Crowley is miffed about the Watergate affair. Such a fuss! And why? Because "armies of enemies" made a "relentless attack on him, even as others commit crimes as egregious and are allowed to survive." Yes, "he helped with his own hanging," but "we claimed his political scalp as a prize to show that those wrenching years [the 1960s] produced at least one ostensibly righteous result. In him, we found a receptacle for all of our self-hatred and misguided upheaval. In his wrongdoing, we found shelter from our own."

Nixon died for our sins?

Well, Crowley is unhampered by experience of the many Nixons who thrived between the Murray Chotiner "pink-slip" campaign against Helen Gahagan Douglas and the "smoking gun." Then, too, given a chance for long, close-up study of an aging historical figure, it would be a strange scholar indeed who spoiled it all by applying a gimlet eye to the old man, and Crowley seems to have been a precocious scholar. In her junior year at Colgate, she wrote Nixon a long, analytical, occasionally critical letter about his book *1999: Victory Without War*. He invited her to visit, was impressed, and hired her to help in his writings on foreign affairs. She thinks he fancied her as a useful instrument for improving his reputation in history:

> I believe he trusted me because he saw me as a liaison between himself and future generations, someone to whom he could tell his story one last time and upon whom he could rely to relate that story to others.... With the end of life coming ever closer, he felt an inescapable need to have his final say before a new generation, to cement the comeback....

Although she must have gussied up Nixon's grammar to eliminate natural conversational stutters, her Nixon sounds like the genuine article. He blusters, fumes, feels sorry for himself, worries about the nation's moral decay, talks trenchantly about politics and foreign affairs, reminisces about old triumphs, repeatedly declares he will not "wallow in Watergate," complains incessantly about the unjust media, and goes on and on about his "enemies," those beloved, hateful, indispensable "enemies" so essential to his view of politics as a blood sport.

"Why do you think people hate me?" he asked Crowley out of the blue one day. Then: "The problem with [then President] Bush is that no one hates him. An effective leader needs enemies because then you know you're doing something right."

Nixon had a positive lust for enemies. One of the more absurd moments of his presidency was the drawing up of the famous "enemies list" of persons who, in the lexicon of the Watergate Nixon, would be "screwed." The person who should have been at the top of the list wasn't even on it. He was, of course, Richard Nixon. As Watergate demonstrated, he was clearly the most deadly enemy he had.

The considerable pleasures of Crowley's book come from the guilty sense that we are eavesdropping while he talks, and talks, and talks to what he believes to be an audience of one. Crowley is not troubled about reporting these confidential conversations. She believes he wanted her to speak to posterity in his behalf, but there is a great deal here that seems delightfully indiscreet for such a secretive man. Did Nixon really want his contempt for President Bush widely broadcast? Poor Bush. As Crowley tells it, he could do nothing to suit Nixon. The old master of foreign policy was outraged by Bush's handling of foreign affairs, and especially about his 1990 friendliness toward the Communist reformer Mikhail Gorbachev in the Soviet Union.

"Has Bush lost his mind?" Nixon asked Crowley when Bush did not try to shake Lithuania out of the Soviet bloc. "... He isn't moving an inch on Lithuania. He just keeps letting his friend Gorbachev roll over the poor place."

Another time: "The guy's got no guts. He just doesn't have it."

And: "I think it's nauseating that the media have proclaimed Bush a newly strong leader." Bush had been "seduced by Gorbachev." He was "too soft on Gorbachev."

Nixon despised Bush's secretary of state, James A. Baker: "Bad news," he called him. "There is no vision there with Bush and certainly not with Baker. Baker was overrated as a strategist, and now he's in totally over his head with foreign policy. He just looks like an amateur out there with [Soviet foreign minister Eduard] Shevardnadze, holding his hand and sounding like he has no backbone. And Bush isn't much better. There is no grand thinking going on over there, no vision. They call it crisis management; I call it lack of leadership."

Even Bush's haberdashery irked Nixon: "I wish Bush wouldn't talk about serious issues looking like he does. They catch him coming off the golf course, no tie, baseball cap—my God! Put on a tie! He should be dressed formally when discussing something as important as this [Soviet relations]. I always wore a suit—perhaps too much. I know it, but I was comfortable in it, and it was appropriate."

Nixon, who made "expletive deleted" a household phrase, was offended by Bush's locker-room talk about Saddam Hussein: "I cannot believe that Bush said 'We'll kick Saddam Hussein's ass.' Can you picture Gorbachev saying 'We'll kick ass in the republics'?"

It would be entertaining to hear him speak with equal candor about Ronald Reagan. It might have been poisonous. Soft as Bush was on Gorbachev, he told Crowley, Reagan would have "gone even farther." This, however, is the only judgment Crowley quotes on the Gipper.

Gerald Ford, his pardoner, receives a brief commendation: "And poor Ford. The pardon was the kiss of death politically, and he still did it. You've got to admire his guts on that score."

Exiled, shamed, and ignored through the Carter, Reagan, and Bush administrations, he was astonished to find the Democrat Clinton extending a friendly hand. Shortly after taking office, Clinton phoned for a forty-minute chat. Crowley suggests Nixon was euphoric.

> ... Most surprising—he confided in me; he said things that he absolutely would not want made public. I wonder if his wire-taps are working!
>
> He was very respectful but with no sickening bullshit. . . . It was the best conversation with a president I've had since I was president. . . . It was never a dialogue with the others. I used to have to force things into the conversation with Reagan and Bush. This was a different cup of tea. . . . This guy does a lot of thinking.

Nixon seized the occasion to preach the importance of foreign policy, the area in which he considered himself a foremost authority. Did he immediately fancy himself becoming Clinton's wise man in foreign policy? "As long as he is talking to me, he'll be OK," he told Crowley. "If he relies on his Carter-type advisers, he will run into trouble."

Clinton invited him to the White House. It was a milestone in the long journey back toward respectability. Reagan and Bush had never done him this symbolic honor.

Eavesdropping, courtesy of Crowley, we learn what he thought of Robert McNamara ("typical elite intellectual type—cold and mean"); of Ted Koppel ("anti-Nixon all the way"); of foreign service officers ("the pits," "all bad," "all liberals, Democrats," but "usually they don't do too much damage"); of United Nations speeches ("worthless, but the media love that fluff"); of domestic economic problems ("let's face it, very boring").

He and Kissinger prolonged the Vietnam War for four years despite his 1968 campaign hints that he had a plan for ending it fast, yet he still despised the antiwar movement: "... To think that I was the one who had to face down those hippie hoodlums who opposed it. My God, I wasn't just from another generation from these people; it was like I was from a different planet." Still, despite those noisy protesters, he told Crowley, most Americans supported his war policy. Didn't his 1972 landslide victory over the dovish George McGovern prove it? Very likely, yes. He was always good on the mechanics of politics. About the rise of the religious right, for instance, he was ambivalent. After the 1992 election, he told Crowley:

> I was disturbed to see that the religious right gained so much momentum. They can contribute very positively to the [Republican] party, and I'm glad they're on our side. But some of their positions, like outlawing abortion, are just too extreme for the United States. They must not be permitted to take over the party or the country. They are too hung up on individual kooky things. I admire their principles but don't think that they should be necessarily put into policy.

During the Anita Hill hearings, he gave Crowley a view of what an old political master might have done. Hill had endangered Senate confirmation of Supreme Court nominee Clarence Thomas with charges of sexual harassment. Thus Nixon to Crowley: "If I were Bush, and Thomas is defeated, and I needed to choose another nominee, I'd stick it to all of them and go for a white woman reactionary card-carrying right-to-lifer! That would drive them crazy!"

Nixon was probably the president with the strongest intellectual instincts since Woodrow Wilson, yet he held intellectuals in contempt. Crowley says he thought them "coldly arrogant" toward "less sophisticated minds." Despite the conservative intellectual movement that was already remaking the Republican Party, he instinctively equated "intellectual" with "liberal Democrat."

Intellectuals are generally not nice people. The modern intellectuals are particularly bad; they're intellectual snobs and hypocrites. The conservatives are cold—they say they don't care, and they don't. The liberals say they care, and they don't. I have more respect for a true-believing Communist than for an American liberal. . . . Most [intellectuals] completely lack courage and have absolutely no heart whatever. . . . Intellectuals hate to admit that they're wrong. And most have led decadent lives; most are moral disasters.

Entertaining as all this faithfully recorded talk may be, there is something a bit eerie about it, too. All the lecturing by one man to a single listener—over 400 pages of it—begins to feel as if it's taking place in an airless, claustrophobic space. There is the sense of a Beckett play in progress: a lonely old man not far from death sits in a room sifting through memories and talking to a young woman. Once he had power to make armies march and millions die, and now he is struggling to persuade himself that he still matters, though he knows he doesn't. Now and then he confronts the reality and emits a cry of despair.

"But will anyone listen?" he asks Crowley. "Will they listen to me anymore?"

Later: "I have been out there talking, but no one in the goddamned administration is listening."

And, to Crowley: "When you go to sleep tonight, remember this: Presidents have some power; former presidents have none!"

After Crowley's claustrophobic Beckett monologue, Stanley I. Kutler's *Abuse of Power*[2] feels like an old-fashioned Warner Brothers gangster film. It opens with the Boss giving an order to the boys: "Goddamnit it, get in and get those files. Blow the safe and get it."

---

2. *Abuse of Power: The New Nixon Tapes* (Free Press, 1997).

The speaker is Nixon. It is 1971. He is President of the United States. Monica Crowley is three years old.

In the very next scene, the Boss is ordering a shakedown of rich people eager to cap their careers with fancy ambassadorships. Of one well-heeled tycoon who yearns to be called "Mister Ambassador," he says, "I want him to be bled for a quarter of a million.... It'll be worth a quarter of a million to just [have to] listen to him...."

A few scenes later: "I'm going to get that Council [on] Foreign Relations. I'm going to chop those bastards off right at the neck."

Nixon connoisseurs will instantly recognize a fresh batch of White House tapes. They have been assembled, annotated, and edited by Kutler, a historian who struggled for years against lawyers and bureaucracies to get all of Nixon's tapes into the public domain. Fewer than forty hours of tapes had been released in 1974; those were enough to force Nixon to resign rather than face impeachment. There were thousands of hours more, however, and Nixon "fought ferociously" to keep them suppressed because, says Kutler, he feared they would damage his attempt to rebuild his reputation. Finally, in 1996, two years after his death, the National Archives and the Nixon Estate agreed to release some 3,700 hours of tapes over a four-year period.

Kutler's *Abuse of Power* consists of the first 201 hours of this previously unpublished material in edited form. The tapes begin with Nixon's curiously outraged reaction to the leaking of the Pentagon Papers in 1971 and continue through the Watergate period until the public learns the tapes exist. They fill a book of more than 600 densely packed pages with a tale at once squalid and absorbing. If Crowley's purpose is to return Nixon to respectability, Kutler's is to drive a stake through his heart.

The argument has never been whether Nixon committed the criminal abuses of power embraced by the term "Watergate." The 1974 tapes were conclusive on that score. The question, as framed by

Nixon's champions, has always been: Were his offenses graver than similar deeds committed by former presidents who didn't have the bad luck to have their every word recorded on tape? Since they all did it, it was unfair to single out Nixon for impeachment. The trouble with this defense is that it's very hard to prove that earlier presidents did, in fact, commit abuses comparable to Nixon's.

Kutler's book leaves no doubt that Nixon was involved from the beginning in the Watergate cover-up. But why? Kutler reads these latest tapes as evidence that Nixon was afraid of what might come out about criminal activities before the Watergate break-in. In his fury about the Pentagon Papers leak, he had created the so-called "plumbers," an assortment of adventurers who were supposed to deal with the leaks that outraged Nixon. Some of their plumbing was very odd indeed.

In one escapade they had broken into a psychiatrist's office searching for a patient's file. The patient was Daniel Ellsberg, who had leaked the Pentagon Papers to *The New York Times*. The "plumbers" were apparently looking for material to damage Ellsberg's reputation. Don't ask how smearing Ellsberg would have diminished the public impact of the Pentagon Papers. We are dealing with people to whom revenge could be its own reward. Talking about Ellsberg to Robert Haldeman, his chief of staff, Nixon said they had to "convict the son of a bitch *in the press. That's the way it's done.*"

The Watergate break-in was a "plumbers" operation. That was in 1972; they had already had a full year of activity. "Plumbers" were among the crew arrested for the Watergate break-in. Suppose they started to talk. People have always wondered why Nixon didn't immediately accept responsibility for the break-in and shrug it off. Kutler believes it was because he knew that one small admission would open Pandora's box, revealing what Attorney General John Mitchell called "the White House horrors."

Breaking in seemed to be a way of doing business at the Nixon

White House. The new tapes show that a year before Watergate, Nixon himself ordered a break-in at the Brookings Institution, a centrist Washington think tank. He thought it held classified material about Pentagon activity: "I want them just to break in and take it out," he tells Haldeman. Then, referring to E. Howard Hunt, who was later to lead the Watergate break-in: "You talk to Hunt. I want the break-in. Hell, they do that. You're to break into the place, rifle the files, and bring them in."

Next morning, learning that the break-in hasn't yet happened, he lectures on the nature of politics:

> These kids don't understand. They have no understanding of politics.... John Mitchell is that way. John is always worried about is it technically correct?... I want you to shake these (unintelligible) up around here. Now you do it. Shake them up. Get them off their Goddamn dead asses.... We're up against an enemy, a conspiracy. They're using any means. We are going to use any means. Is that clear?

This fresh group of tapes may be of more interest to historians and law students than to the general reader, but it contains hundreds of entertaining glimpses of life in the Oval Office as a president feels his power crumbling away. We learn, for example, that Nixon kept Senator Ted Kennedy under surveillance for nine months to learn about his "after-hours" activities. "Just might get lucky and catch this sonofabitch and grill him for '76," Nixon muses.

There is Nixon's strange obsession with Lawrence O'Brien, the Democratic national chairman, in whose office the Watergate burglars were arrested. O'Brien is targeted for an IRS tax audit. "We wanted to rummage through the records," Haldeman explains. It was 1972, and O'Brien asked that the audit be postponed until after the election. Request denied, Haldeman reports. Nixon: "That's a lot of nerve, to say to put it off until after the election." Later, Haldeman reports the IRS hit "a dry hole."

By the summer of 1973, with the cover-up collapsing, Nixon becomes furious at Senator Howard Baker. Baker is the ranking Republican on the Senate Select Committee, which is systematically demolishing Nixon's defense. Baker's objective stance has irritated Nixon for weeks; now his temper explodes. Senator Sam Ervin, the committee's Democratic chairman, suggests that he and Baker come to the White House for a conference.

"I said I would talk to him [Ervin] alone," Nixon says. "Otherwise, we'll get that simpering asshole Baker down here.... I'm not gonna let him come in."

Fifteen minutes later:

> ...Now Howard Baker...never be in the White house again— never, never, never.... He will never be on a presidential plane again.... Now I screwed him today.... Ervin...said he and Baker he wanted to come, I said, "Oh, no," I said, "I'll see you alone. Baker is not going to be here again." ...I don't want anybody in the White House to ever have any contact with him again. Ever. And another thing is this: cut him off. Give him a deep freeze.

That same day Henry Kissinger comes to the Oval Office with good news. He has just had a phone call from Norman Mailer, who is doing an article on Watergate. "Well, he says...for the first time in his life, he's beginning to like you." At this point only a person with a heart of stone can possibly laugh.

After so much about the bizarre aspects of Nixon's personality, Allen J. Matusow reminds us that there was far more to his presidency than scandal. It is easy to forget that, while struggling with Watergate, he was also at grips with complex economic problems, including the worst recession of the postwar years. Professor Matusow's economic history of the Nixon years, *Nixon's Economy*,[3] is remarkable not only for the subtlety with which he analyzes Nixon's economic predicament, but also for a clear and graceful prose that makes it a pleasure to read.

The predicament was that Nixon "happened to occupy the presidency at the moment when the postwar boom ground to a permanent halt." From the outset, he had to deal with "economic traumas more severe than anything known since the Great Depression." The economy was faltering by the end of his first year in office. During the time of Watergate, he confronted worldwide food shortages, an unprecedented oil crisis, double-digit inflation, and the worst recession of the postwar years.

At the end of 1971 it seemed possible that a depressed economy could destroy his hopes for reelection. Matusow's book details the twists and turns with which he tried to avoid this. It was a cruel trial for Nixon, who was illiterate in economics and, moreover, bored by the subject. His search for experts' advice finally turned up the unlikely John Connally, one-time protégé of Lyndon Johnson and now a Democrat for Nixon. Nixon made him secretary of the treasury and took such an astonishing liking to him that he ultimately said Connally was the only man qualified to succeed him in the presidency.

As an economist, Connally proved disastrous. He was influential in persuading Nixon to do the unprecedented by imposing wage and price controls in peacetime. That failed. Connally's bellicose call for a showdown in world trade, if anything, probably deepened the troubles of American exporters. He proposed to force open foreign markets with punitive measures against nations that refused to cut back their exports to America. In this "get-tough-with-the-world" policy, Matusow says, Connally and his colleague Peter Peterson of the

---

3. *Nixon's Economy: Booms, Busts, Dollars, and Votes* (University Press of Kansas, 1998).

Council for International Economic Policy "nearly wrecked the world trade system."

Matusow is especially good on Nixon as politician. Neither liberal nor conservative, he was out to preempt the center of American politics by building a "New Majority." The old majority was Democratic, forged by Franklin Roosevelt, and consisted of an alliance between Southern conservatives, labor, and Northern liberals. Like the one-horse shay, it was ready to fall to pieces, and Nixon sensed it.

> In addition to social conservatism, waving the flag, and playing the race card, Nixon sought center ground by judicious expansion of the welfare state. It was no part of Nixon's initial purpose to cut taxes or slash expenditures, as conservatives were urging. He knew that spending money was more popular than pinching pennies, and he favored balancing the budget only so long as it did not cost him votes.

To convert labor, he courted George Meany, leader of the AFL-CIO. He adopted a destructive policy of imposing quotas on Japanese imports in order to satisfy the old Dixiecrat Strom Thurmond, who was vital to his plans for capturing the South. Thurmond's South Carolina textile mills were suffering under Japanese competition.

Nixon never fails to surprise us. Thus, for example, Matusow, having apparently hacked his way through the impenetrable *Haldeman Diaries*, finds Nixon talking about creating a new party with Connally's help:

> Following the November elections, the two of them would move to build a new political party, the Independent Conservative Party, "or something of that sort," that would include Southern and other conservative Democrats, along with middle "road to conservative Republicans."

By the end of Nixon's second term, they could dramatically change the country's entire political structure. "The candidate of the new party in 1976 would be John Connally."

Perhaps Nixon was just schmoozing here with Haldeman. He was a masterful political tactician. Surely he couldn't have believed that the country was ready for another Texan in the White House so soon after Lyndon Johnson.

Chapter 8

THE LOVE BOAT

AT THE END when everything was crashing down around him William Shawn seems to have been an authentically tragic figure. Hundreds of artists and writers were prepared to attest to his nobility and did so frequently without being asked. He was nearly eighty years old when the fall came and had been editor of *The New Yorker* for thirty-five years. He had been picked for the job by Harold Ross, the magazine's founder and first editor, and he took command in 1952 shortly after Ross died. The magazine staff, a band of fractious individualists who agreed on little else, accepted Shawn without the faintest rumble of discontent. It seemed the universal opinion that he was the ideal choice for the job.

"Great" is a heavily overworked word among Americans, and for this reason was not used casually at *The New Yorker*, with its distaste for overstatement and tired adjectives. Soon, however, *New Yorker* people began calling Shawn "a great editor," and some flirted with heresy by suggesting that he was superior even to the sainted Harold Ross. James Thurber, one of *The New Yorker*'s gods, praised him in his cranky memoir, *The Years with Ross*.[1] Several good things had happened to Ross in 1933, Thurber wrote. For one, "God sent him William

---

1. Atlantic/Little, Brown, 1957.

Shawn." At the onset of World War II Ross made Shawn his chief deputy. "Without Shawn's hard work and constant counsel," Thurber wrote, "Ross would never have made the distinguished record he did as editor during the war."

From Thurber, who with E. B. White helped create the distinctive *New Yorker* voice, this was high praise. Not high enough, however, for Shawn's devotees, according to Ved Mehta, himself a Shawn admirer. Mehta subtitled his 1998 memoir in praise of Shawn "The Invisible Art of Editing," suggesting that Shawn had transcended mere journalism and become an artist.[2] He describes a party at Shawn's apartment in the 1960s at which other guests were denigrating Thurber and his recently published book on Ross. Edith Oliver, who reviewed off-Broadway theater for the magazine, is quoted saying, "The book is trash.... It's all untrue," and "Thurber is a horse's ass."

"'His work has really been falling off,' Naomi [Bliven] put in." She was a *New Yorker* book reviewer. Another woman said she had run into Thurber at the Algonquin Hotel, a favorite haunt of the *New Yorker* set, and heard him "saying an awful lot of bitter things about Bill [Shawn] and *The New Yorker*'s fiction department."

Mehta apparently looked shocked by this vituperation, for he reports that Shawn's eighteen-year-old son Wallace took him aside to explain that "old-timers at *The New Yorker* really, um, hate Thurber's book." It glorified Ross and "scarcely even mentions Dad." Mehta was writing all this some thirty-five years after the party, so one cannot help wondering about the reliability of his memory, even though he could still recall Wallace emitting that "um." Still, gang backbitings like this have always been common in the publishing trades.

Shawn, who was famous for shyness and dislike of confrontation, seems to have been embarrassed by the incident and ended it graciously with a small lecture, which Mehta remembers this way:

2. *Remembering Mr. Shawn's New Yorker: The Invisible Art of Editing* (Overlook, 1998).

"Thurber, together with [S. J.] Perelman, has to be one of the greatest humorists of our century," Mr. Shawn was saying... [and] went on to give examples of Thurber's funny writing....

"Of course Thurber is a great genius," Edith said, for the first time sounding calm. Her transformation under Mr. Shawn's gentle prompting was remarkable.

What is striking about Mehta's account is the sense it conveys of the group's devotion to Shawn. They may rage against those who deny him his due share of praise, but they quickly become calm and gentle as he subtly steers them toward a more generous, more civilized view of Thurber. He was an editor in complete control of a staff utterly devoted to him.

In later years this devotion came to be expressed by some of his admirers as "love." Here was a strange evolution at a magazine famous for despising sentimentality. A loved editor is a rare beast anywhere in the publishing trades. Many editors are admired, but there is something eerie about an editor being loved. Editors do cruel things to the submissions of writers and cartoonists. Often they throw the work back into the submitter's face, declaring it unfit to print. Even when condescending to accept it they demand rewriting, restructuring, and slashing that often seem to turn the artist's or cartoonist's work into someone else's. It is unnatural to love someone who commits these cruelties on one's creative work; no editing matched *The New Yorker*'s for thoroughness.

Yet here are 414 pages by Mehta which amount to a declaration of love for Shawn—"the legendary, saintly, canonical Mr. Shawn," as Renata Adler calls him. And here is an astonishing memoir by Lillian Ross announcing for all the world to know that she loved Shawn and that Shawn loved her back with such vigor for so many years that she regarded herself as his wife.[3] Hers is a love so overpowering

---

3. *Here But Not Here* (Random House, 1998).

that she must shout it out, regardless of any pain it might cause Shawn's wife and sons. Brendan Gill also loved Shawn. His *Here at The New Yorker*, published in 1975, is now reissued with a new introduction that Gill wrote in 1997.[4] When Shawn occasionally sent him a memo of thanks for performing some small favor and the memo ended "'With love,' then how grateful I had reason to be. For like everyone else on the magazine, I felt a desire, childish as it unquestionably was, to be a Shawn favorite, and even, still more childishly, to be first among his favorites." What a bizarre confession. One thinks of Proust's sleepless young Marcel yearning for Maman to come and kiss him good night.

Renata Adler's memoir *Gone*[5] is a turmoil of confused emotions. Oh, she loves Shawn all right. While recalling a somewhat tense business meeting with Shawn, she interrupts herself to say, "This may be an odd place to say that I loved him. I did love him." This is not Adler's only reference to love. Near the end of her book Shawn is fired and Adler gives *The New York Times* a comment that infuriates Lillian Ross —the "office wife," as Adler calls her—prompting Ross to tell her, "You've lost the respect of the people who love you here."

As often happens when love is afoot, it became the source of considerable ill temper among people at the magazine. Adler's love for Shawn makes it impossible for her to contain her outrage for Lillian Ross's claim to have been the most thoroughly loved of all his admirers, or, in Gill's phrase, the "first among his favorites." Ross's reveries about thirty years of idyllic love with Shawn succeed only in persuading Adler that, far from loving him, Ross unconsciously "disliked and even despised him." Ross's book turns Shawn into "an unctuous, pompous, humorless creep, whose greatness is revealed in his feeling for her—and his dislike and disdain for everybody else."

---

4. Da Capo, 1997.
5. *Gone: The Last Days of The New Yorker* (Simon and Schuster, 1999).

After Shawn's firing, Adler pays a last visit to his office. "First of all," she tells him, "it goes without saying, I love you and I hope to keep seeing you for the rest of our lives." Shawn interrupts, saying "'I love you' quite firmly." In their conversation they are "sometimes crying, sometimes not." Finally Adler rises, goes to the door to leave, and Shawn says "in a tone of surprising firmness and, considering the distance, gentleness, 'I love you.' I said again that I loved him...."

Poor Shawn. All that love, all that respect. It became the custom to call him "Mister Shawn." To people who didn't know him it made him sound quaint and schoolmasterish. He wasn't. That "Mister" marked him as an extraordinary man of respect in a publishing world where the most august figures were called simply by nicknames or ungarnished last names. Henry Luce was always just plain "Luce," except in the presence of course. Shawn's predecessor was not "Mr. Ross" but always "Ross." Even at *The New York Times*, a model of propriety in such matters, "Mister" had become archaic. Turner Catledge, its managing editor, was "Turner," and James Reston, its Washington main man, was "Scotty." The publisher, Arthur O. Sulzberger, remained a breezy "Punch," even in his presence. "Mister" was an antique form applied only to the revered Adolph Ochs, dead long before most living *Times* people had left their playpens.

To old-timers of the Harold Ross era at *The New Yorker*, "Mister Shawn" had been simply "Shawn" or "Bill." Now, though, as he settled into Ross's job and did it exceedingly well, new people at the magazine gradually turned him into "Mister Shawn." Adler's memoir calls him "Mr. Shawn" throughout. So does Mehta's remembrance of what he calls "Mr. Shawn's *New Yorker*." Only Lillian Ross calls him "Bill," thus asserting her primacy on the love ladder. Probably Shawn did not encourage the Mistering. Still the old-fashioned politeness of it spoke of something he was trying to preserve in the magazine. It might strike an up-to-date, with-it generation as musty, but it also declared that civility and politeness still mattered at *The New Yorker*.

This was a daring attitude to strike after the 1960s when civility and politeness came to be viewed more and more as quaint remnants of a reactionary generation whose time had passed. Shawn and his *New Yorker* were struggling against a tide that threatened to sweep civility and politeness out of American life. In his old age he was to pay dearly for it.

In a spate of books whose appearance is timed to coincide with the magazine's seventy-fifth birthday, it is Ben Yagoda's *About Town*[6] that best explains what made Shawn a superb editor. There was, first, a capacity for taking infinite pains to achieve precision. Although his personal manner was shy, gentle, and withdrawn, almost apologetic, he could become ruthless when working on a manuscript. Out went every bit of "extraneous, repetitive, or discordant material." In their place Shawn inserted "just the right word, phrase, or sentence" that improved the piece. Sometimes he could leave a manuscript looking brutalized. In editing an article by Matthew Josephson, a successful writer of the 1940s, Shawn "virtually disassembled" the piece; not a single line remained as Josephson had written it until the middle of the fourth page.

Writers not only put up with these assaults, but also thanked Shawn for committing them. Almost invariably they conceded that Shawn's editing had improved their work without changing its content. S. N. Behrman, after working with Shawn on profiles of the playwright Ferenc Molnár and the art dealer Joseph Duveen, was lyrical in praise of the results. Though the work had been hard and exhausting, it had "been wonderful also and chiefly because of Shawn's collaboration," Behrman wrote. "He has a passion for perfection, which is so rare in this sloppy age, and what he has contributed to the pieces is, literally, more than I could possibly compute. He is one of the rarest and subtlest minds I have ever encountered."

---

6. *About Town: The New Yorker and the World It Made* (Scribner, 2000).

Not every writer was so enchanted by a Shawn editing. After a few experiences, Margaret Case Harriman complained to Harold Ross that "it never used to be such a life-work, such a disheartening, endless, joyless, *boring* pain in the neck to correct proofs." But malcontents were few. Yagoda estimates that between sixty and eighty *New Yorker* writers have dedicated books to Shawn. Yagoda suggests that Shawn the tigerish editor got away with his aggressions because the staff "could not but respond to his profound attention, strong respect for, and unabashed flattery of their work." He loved them, and they loved him back.

In personal encounters Shawn apparently couldn't bring himself to speak hard truths to writers. Rather than tell a writer his piece wasn't good enough, he often bought it and put it in deep storage with dozens of other pieces destined never to reach the newsstands because Shawn didn't think them good enough but hated to tell their authors. He was creating a workplace without much stimulus for writers to produce. The self-starters didn't mind, but others wrote less and less, and two of the magazine's best—Joseph Mitchell and J. D. Salinger—stopped writing entirely.

Was Shawn's perfectionism a factor behind writer's block? Mehta says he had written swiftly and easily in the past,

> but now that I was at *The New Yorker* I seemed to be incapable of writing even a letter off the top of my head. As soon as I put down a sentence, I saw problems with it and started over. By the end of the day, I often didn't have even one sentence that I liked, and answering a handful of letters sometimes took me most of a week. In the meantime, I could get no other [writing] work done, and felt like a taxi-driver going up and down the avenue with his meter running but without a fare.

Well, Harold Ross had also been a perfectionist nuisance. In this regard Shawn had made no vital change. In important ways, though, he changed Ross's *New Yorker* significantly. Ross had wanted *New Yorker* pieces to be short. Shawn was more interested in complicated journalistic stories that took a lot of space to tell, and he was willing to let them run. And run and run, in the later stages of his career. Still, he published some astonishingly good journalism. Reporting had been important to the magazine in Ross's time. When World War II made it hard for *The New Yorker* to continue thriving on its reputation as a humor magazine, Ross began publishing serious work by foreign correspondents writing from world capitals and battle fronts.

Shawn was his indispensable right-hand man during this change of course. After the war it was Shawn who persuaded Ross to devote an entire issue exclusively to publication of John Hersey's *Hiroshima*. It doesn't "hold up very well," Renata Adler writes in *Gone*, thereby missing the point. *Hiroshima* was journalism, and journalism is not supposed to hold up; it is supposed to deliver the news. Hersey delivered it with stunning impact at a time when America was still almost entirely ignorant of what a nuclear bombing implied.

Yagoda's book is also good on Ross, but *Letters from the Editor* is even better.[7] It gives us Ross living and breathing. The book is an assortment of Ross's letters, never intended for publication. Ross was obviously a natural writer, but he never wrote for his magazine, or aspired to. He would probably have rejected his own writing as unsuitable, for his prose was loud, muscular, and vulgar, and he wanted his magazine's voice to be subdued, delicate, and polite. What's more, he hated writers trying to inject themselves into their work, and Ross's letters are so filled with Ross that by the end of this collection the reader seems to have met him in person. And had a wonderful time.

Temperamentally, Ross and Shawn came from opposite poles. Shawn hated rejecting work; Ross did it with gusto. When William

---

7. *Letters from the Editor: The New Yorker's Harold Ross*, edited by Thomas Kunkel (Modern Library, 2000).

Rose Benét submits a poem, Ross bounces back a note saying, "We like your stuff, God knows, but this verse, damn it, is obscure."

E. B. White's father dies, and there is no writer more important to Ross than White, but his letter of condolence discloses a man utterly incapable of syrupy pieties: "Was very sorry to hear about your father, and send my sympathy, which is about all I have to say, except that after you get to be thirty people you know keep dropping off all the time and it's a hell of a note."

Despite their differing personalities, Shawn's editorship was governed to the very end by Ross's principles. Even in the 1980s, when custom and the Supreme Court had authorized wholesale use of what Ross once called "daring words," Shawn refused to allow them in the magazine. Ross had always hated them, and Shawn upheld the code. Ross discussed his policy in a letter to Frank Crowninshield, the editor of *Vanity Fair*, in 1933:

> I am an old-fashioned double-standard boy who is shocked at nothing, absolutely nothing, in a stag gathering, but who is embarrassed poignantly at any word or reference which used to be called off-color in mixed company.... The hell of it is that in these days of disillusionment, when fathers insist that they want their daughters to have "experience before marriage" and when Vassar graduates turn up with a vocabulary which you haven't heard since the old days in Fanny Brown's hook shop in California, I don't know how to gauge the standards of mixed company....
>
> Sometimes in fiction stories and where the writer is entitled to considerable privilege, we let "Christ" go through; "bitch" probably yes; "bastard" I would shrink at. I have argued three or four "bastards" out of print in the last three or four months....

The magazine's resistance to he-man prose endured throughout Shawn's tenure. Younger writers complained that it showed the magazine was no longer in the cultural mainstream. Marketers worried about declining ad revenue and circulation argued that the policy made the magazine seem too old-fashioned to interest young consumers. The antique gates were finally opened by Robert Gottlieb and Tina Brown, who edited the magazine after Shawn's departure, and the old Anglo-Saxon synonyms for body excretions, sexual congress, and reproductive organs flowed in at last. Thus ended the age of Ross and Shawn.

Renata Adler's *Gone* is up to more than such a small book can deliver. It is a sob of mourning for the passing of the Ross-Shawn *New Yorker*, and an angry attempt to settle old scores with a few former colleagues, and a cry of frustration about time's insistence on moving on to the next thing. To mourn the death of the old *New Yorker* is, after all, to complain because the world changes and because people and things we love grow old, fail, and die.

Splendid though he had been, her Mr. Shawn had begun to lose his grip. She reports as much from personal observation. It should have been expected by a man as astute as Shawn. He was approaching eighty and should have known that octogenarians cannot go on and on. If he didn't then it was surely time for him to step aside. The magazine had entered an era in which almost everything had become as impermanent as a firefly on a June night. In this hopped-up culture, *The New Yorker*, which stood against all things hopped-up, was becoming hard pressed to find a commercially important audience.

There are many versions of Shawn's endgame. Adler may love Shawn, but she is not kind to him in her account of the fall. She seems to think that the magazine (Shawn, one supposes) had become dangerously filled with sinful pride in its own integrity:

> ...The downside of this integrity was becoming this: a moral certitude, an absence of self-doubt—especially in political

matters—that became a minor flaw and then a major flaw, which led, I believe, to the eventual dissolution of the magazine.... What had been a place of originality and integrity began to publish, and defend, instances of false reporting and plagiarism. What had been a place of civility, tact, understatement, became a place of vulgarity, meanness, invasions of privacy.

She is even harder on Shawn's attempts to pick a successor. As time passed and many were mentioned and none was chosen, she concludes that Shawn "never had the slightest intention" of making way for a successor. Shawn inspired office speculation from time to time about staff editors being chosen to succeed him, but Adler thought it was all fakery, a charade to persuade the staff—"and perhaps himself"—that he intended "permitting the magazine to survive him."

In her view, and she is persuasive, Shawn had become so determined to hang on that he was toying with his editors' ambitions in order to keep himself in the editor's chair. We are left to infer that senility was beginning to distort his judgment. The staff realized that something was going wrong. Roger Angell, the fiction editor, wrote E. B. White, his stepfather, that Shawn "has been unable to delegate *anything*, and he has become suspicious and overexcited and even a bit paranoid about any discussion having to do with his successor or his retirement."

He seems to have been surprised when, in 1984, the Fleischmann interests who owned a controlling share of the magazine sold it to Advance Communications, a giant publishing conglomerate operating a group of successful popular magazines through Condé Nast. S. I. Newhouse, the new owner, seemed to hit it off with Shawn and let him stay on, supposedly to pick a successor. Adler's description of Shawn at this stage suggests a tragic Lear-like figure, a dithering old man, once master of his world, now shocked when Newhouse, in 1987, fires him.

A last sadly comic act was played out in *The New Yorker* offices the day Shawn received his pink slip. Most of the staff assembled in an office corridor to express their natural shock and their devotion to Shawn. Lillian Ross was "in command," Adler recalls, and soon the group was being stampeded into action, which, these being writers, meant composing a letter. While the discussion ran on, Adler says Shawn himself several times declared, "The magazine is in jeopardy."

Newhouse had appointed Robert Gottlieb, chief editor at Knopf, to Shawn's job, and the meeting decided to send Gottlieb a letter urging him not to accept it. "This preposterous letter," as Adler called it, was composed by a committee and signed, according to Yagoda, by 153 people, and Gottlieb, of course, took the job anyway.

Shawn apparently expected those who had signed to quit the magazine when he left, and he was hurt when most chose to keep their jobs. He had "asked them for a token gesture of solidarity, and they had said no to him," Lillian Ross writes. Mehta says Shawn "actually believed that, as Gottlieb came over, all of us who had signed the protest letter would go down in the elevator and never come back."

Shawn's farewell letter to his staff spoke of love:

> ...We have built something quite wonderful together. Love has been the controlling emotion, and love is the essential word. *The New Yorker*, as a reader once said, has been the gentlest of magazines. Perhaps it has also been the greatest, but that matters far less. What matters most is that you and I, working together, taking strength from the inspiration that our first editor, Harold Ross, gave us, have tried constantly to find and say what is true. I must speak of love once more. I love all of you, and will love you as long as I live.

He lived to be eighty-five. In the vital years of his manhood he had cherished his dignity and his privacy. After his death, those who claimed to love him seem to have thought, his dignity and privacy no longer mattered. They began to write books.

Chapter 9

MR. RIGHT

1.

BARRY GOLDWATER LOVED ham radio and liked to fly airplanes, was a fine photographer, had a lifelong subscription to *Popular Mechanics*, inherited a share of his family's department store, and as a retailer became celebrated as the creator of "antsy-pants," men's boxer shorts imprinted with drawings of ants crawling this way and that. He was a man's man, a guy's guy, a regular fellow. Big, handsome, square-jawed, quick to smile, easy to like. A straight-from-the-shoulder talker who'd rather tinker with his old souped-up car than go to a black-tie dinner.

Make him a presidential candidate running against the shrewdest politician who ever cut a deal, and you have a movie by Frank Capra: *Mr. Goldwater Runs for President*. Capra's Goldwater of course would have won. American innocents were Capra's specialty, and they never lost. Whether they went to whorish, thieving Washington like Mr. Smith or went to town playing the tuba like "pixillated" Mr. Deeds, they prevailed. In Capra's America innocence could never be defeated.

The real Goldwater was not quite so innocent as that. He surely knew all along that he was going to lose to Lyndon Johnson in 1964. Anybody who ran against Johnson was probably going to lose that year, because Johnson held a nearly unbeatable hand. People who watched Goldwater campaign suspected, however, that he was a little too resigned to losing, that maybe he really didn't want to win. One afternoon while campaigning by train in the Middle West he climbed into the engineer's cab, took control of the locomotive, and hauled his own rented train across the prairie. That was not what a man did who had "fire in the belly," as the reporters called the consuming lust for presidential power; it was Goldwater the *Popular Mechanics* subscriber extracting at least one boyish adventure from this miserable experience.

Long afterward Goldwater wrote that he had been "better equipped, psychologically" for military life than for politics. "If I had my life to live over again, I'd go to West Point," he said in his autobiography. Well, he was nearly eighty when he wrote that and maybe losing touch with the man he had been when young. The evidence suggests he would not have flourished under military discipline. As a young Republican senator he once attacked a Republican president, a five-star general named Eisenhower, for operating "a dime-store New Deal." Such insubordination spoke of a man more passionate about politics than discipline.

Perhaps he was one of those politicians who are born not to command but to preach crusades. He was a good talker, but not much for doing. "Lazy" was the judgment of reporters who covered him in the Senate. When he talked, though, audiences cheered and opened their checkbooks.

The gospel he preached was "conservatism." Forty years ago it was a word no politician had spoken, except with contempt, since the age of the Hoover collar. Nowadays of course politicians fling it about with the same reverence accorded "home" and "mother," but by the late 1950s Goldwater was saying "conservative" with a bravado that unnerved many Republicans and roused many more to a fresh passion for politics. His 1964 campaign was to bring the word out of shame and darkness. Despite his humiliating defeat, "conservatism" soon became the battle cry of shrewd and angry political newcomers who gutted the old Republican Party and rebuilt today's model on a foundation of Sunbelt millions, old-time religion, and white Southern solidarity.

Rick Perlstein's richly detailed history, *Before the Storm*,[1] makes it clear that Goldwater was pathetically and sometimes comically out of his depth as a presidential candidate. We revisit the fiasco of his acceptance speech and his choice of upstate New York congressman William Miller, a man unknown outside the party and unloved within, as his vice-presidential candidate. Instead of trying to heal wounds created by the nasty struggle for the nomination, Goldwater goes along with a convention eager to shoot the wounded. This ensures an enduring party split while treating a national television audience to a hair-raising spectacle of conservatives as a dangerous mob howling at Nelson Rockefeller.

Finally, in an act of supreme folly, he refuses to give control of his campaign to F. Clifton White, the brilliant political technician who has got him the nomination, and hands it instead to some unqualified friends from back home in Arizona.

Only a liberal with a sadist's heart can take pleasure in Goldwater's anguish: he was a decent man trapped by events in the wrong job. Six years later, Perlstein notes, Goldwater described his 1964 role in a way suggesting he thought of himself as a victim of history:

> Very early in the [1960s] I found myself becoming a political fulcrum of the vast and growing tide of American disenchantment with the public policies of liberalism.... It is true that I sensed it early and sympathized with it publicly, but I did not originate it.... I was caught up in and swept along by this tide of disenchantment.

---

1. *Before the Storm: Barry Goldwater and the Unmaking of the American Consensus* (Hill and Wang, 2001).

As Perlstein observes: "There it was: controlled by events, following others' call, a horse to be ridden."

But there was no other horse available. The point to remember about Goldwater is that he was all there was. In 1964 Ronald Reagan had not yet reinvented himself as the most charming politician since Franklin Roosevelt. Except for Goldwater, not a single conservative Republican was a remotely plausible presidential candidate. Inept he may have been and lacking in guile, but he was at least presentable. The Senate had a large group of conservative Republicans until the 1958 elections, when the spread of television campaigning tempted them to show themselves on camera. Their audiences must have found them painful to the eye, for nearly all were turned out of office, and Democrats took the Senate by a landslide.

Judging a politician by his looks may be absurd, but the fact is undeniable: a nifty profile and a cheerful countenance carry great weight with American voters. Conservatism in those years seemed to afflict its leaders with hard and angry faces. Goldwater was the exception. He had the smile of a genial neighbor. When he became angry it was not the silent fury of the John Bircher who believed President Eisenhower was a crypto-Communist; it was the exasperated cry of a man telling the world he's mad as hell with bureaucrats interfering in his business and he's not going to take it anymore.

Perlstein's book begins with the people who recognized Goldwater early in the game as the only possible candidate and set out to snare him. Clarence Manion, the disillusioned New Dealer who had become dean of the Notre Dame law school, gets a great deal of attention. So do William Rusher and William F. Buckley, founders of the *National Review*, which was to become the intellectual showcase for Goldwater-style conservatism.

The tempting of Goldwater is told in detail. Goldwater resists, then only pretends to resist, then finds he has a taste for the thing, gradually starts to relent, but protests and protests as every manipulation moves him deeper into the campaign. L. Brent Bozell, Buckley's college classmate, rushes to patch together a book from Goldwater's old speeches. Goldwater, having left college after his freshman year and lacking both the skill and the appetite for composition, cannot be expected to write his own book, and a conservative candidate needs a book expounding his conservative ideology. Bozell gets it written. Titled *The Conscience of a Conservative*, it becomes a best seller.

Whether the book is more Bozell than Goldwater is unclear. Perlstein says Goldwater "skimmed Bozell's manuscript and pronounced it fine." Read today, it speaks with an innocent brashness rare in American politics. It assumes that American society is in a dangerous decline because Republicans as well as Democrats have lost respect for the Constitution and refuse to take the simple, if radical, steps necessary to make America whole again.

The conservative's goal, it states, is to provide "the maximum amount of freedom for individuals that is consistent with the maintenance of social order." And so, for example, the conservative would abolish farm subsidies, thus freeing the farmer to share the same free-market challenges that other Americans face. The conservative would abolish the graduated income tax and restore equality by taxing everyone, pauper and Croesus, at the same rate. The federal government would stop "profligate" spending projects, including social welfare, education, public power, public housing, and urban-renewal programs.

While Goldwater always personally endorsed school desegregation, his book maintained that the Supreme Court had no constitutional power to order it since education was the exclusive province of state and local governments.

In foreign policy, the book foresaw Soviet communism winning the cold war because a "craven fear of death" had entered the American psyche. America was easily bullied because it was too afraid of nuclear war. Here came a burst of bellicose prose of the sort Democrats would gleefully exploit: "We must—as the first step toward saving American freedom—...make it the cornerstone of our foreign policy: that we would rather die than lose our freedom."

That Goldwater won the nomination despite this assault on the status quo may simply mean that Americans don't take campaign books seriously enough to read them closely. Whatever the case, its unorthodoxies did not raise serious problems for Goldwater until the nomination was well in hand.

In Perlstein's telling, the hero of the nomination campaign was F. Clifton White. It was White who first saw that the Republican nomination was available for the taking by whoever could master "the occult process" by which Republicans chose their candidates and their "Rube Goldberg–like system" for selecting convention delegates.

White was less interested in ideology than in the calculus of practical politics. A quiet backroom operator from upstate New York, he received his elementary political education in the 1940s while being outmaneuvered by Communists during a struggle for control of a veterans lobbying group. He became fascinated by the mechanics of acquiring power through democratic process. Why he signed on to elect Goldwater is unclear. Maybe he simply wanted to see if he could pull it off.

White's strategy assumed a force of Goldwater supporters more passionate about "saving Western Civilization" than about getting patronage rewards, Perlstein writes.

> Their work would begin at the dewiest grassroots level, recruiting and training candidates to stand for election to the precinct conventions; those people, in turn, would select delegates to county conventions; these, finally, would choose the national convention delegates.

States that wanted favorite-son nominations were to be encouraged.

A favorite-son delegation could become a powerful Trojan horse if all the members were really gung-ho for Goldwater. Sometimes it paid to look weak. That made you more intimidating once you proved yourself strong.

It was just as Clif White learned from the Communists—and also from John F. Kennedy's Irish Mafia, who had started working the precincts shortly after the 1956 [Democratic] convention. A single small organization, from a distance and with minimal resources, working in stealth, could take on an entire party.

Lisa McGirr's *Suburban Warriors*[2] affords a rare picture of the grassroots process actually working at a specific site very much as White had envisioned it. McGirr's setting is California's Orange County, which became America's most celebrated conservative stronghold in the 1960s. Its fame came from its reputation for being what *Fortune* magazine called political "nut country." (Its congressman James Utt made news in 1963 by suggesting that "a large contingent of barefooted Africans" might be training in Georgia as part of a United Nations military exercise to take over the United States.) McGirr's book provides a valuable scholarly analysis of the demographics, culture, and history that made the county distinctively "conservative."

At the start of the Goldwater movement the county was a place of white middle-class suburbanites recently settled into new tract housing developments. Its people were well educated, held high-tech jobs, and tended to see their prosperity as the result of entrepreneurial economics, despite Southern California's dependence on the federally financed military-industrial complex. Many were migrants from Midwestern states that had been "steeped in nationalism, moralism, and piety." They tended to think the republic was in political, economic, and moral decline, and to blame the liberal tradition for it.

---

2. Princeton University Press, 2001.

McGirr's account suggests an old-fashioned, Midwestern, small-town culture resettled in a dynamic new consumer society by the Pacific. While acknowledging that Orange County had bizarre aspects, she suggests that basically it was as American as Warren G. Harding dreaming of a return to "normalcy." Liberals who experienced Orange County passion firsthand may think it was not quite so pastoral.

White started working on the Goldwater nomination in 1961. When the Republicans assembled in the San Francisco Cow Palace in the summer of 1964, he had beaten the once formidable moderate Northeastern establishment which had ruled party conventions seemingly forever. That summer its leaders included former President Eisenhower, the all-purpose Massachusetts aristocrat Henry Cabot Lodge, and Governors Rockefeller of New York, Scranton of Pennsylvania, and Romney of Michigan. They had fretted, fidgeted, and fought indecisively among themselves all year about who the nominee should be. They were backing Rockefeller when a baby was born to his new wife on the eve of the California primary. This revived at the worst possible moment the scandal of his divorce, and two days later Goldwater won the California election. There was a futile last-minute attempt to stop Goldwater by rallying a coalition behind Scranton, and White easily snuffed it out.

Perlstein's account of what happened next is an ancient tale of triumph as the father of disaster. In this supreme moment Goldwater had an acceptance speech to give. After such a nasty convention, precedent called for a conciliatory bromide about burying anger in brotherhood and marching onward to the White House. Goldwater didn't feel like doing that.

He and his closest advisors rejected conciliation. They thought that neither Scranton nor Rockefeller deserved conciliation. Goldwater asked for a draft speech from Harry Jaffa, a political science professor and Abraham Lincoln expert from Ohio State University who held that if Lincoln were then alive he would call himself a conservative.

Perlstein says Jaffa wanted to do something with the word "extremism." Democrats were using it to make voters think Goldwater was a war-crazed wild man too reckless to be trusted with the nuclear button. "Goldwater was sick of the word." His "brain trust," as Perlstein calls them, quarreled over one of Jaffa's lines. Too incendiary, some argued. Goldwater liked it. He ordered it underlined twice. Thus the origin of the most famous speech of the campaign.

The text of the finished speech was so closely held that Goldwater's chief political strategists, including White, were not allowed an advance peek, for fear that would "raise hell," says Perlstein. Nowadays Goldwater's underlined words seem nothing more than a bland philosophical observation that a good cause is better pursued with "extremism" than with "moderation": "*I would remind you that extremism in the defense of liberty—is—no—vice!*" A roar of approval interrupted him for forty seconds. Then: "*And let me remind you also—that moderation in the pursuit of justice is no virtue!*"

Gentle philosophizing was not what Goldwater had in mind. He knew very well that "extremism" and "moderation" were explosive words that year. He was telling the party that he had no interest in trying to preserve the old middle-of-the-road consensus. He was telling the "moderates" they could choke on their own frustration.

"A cultural call to arms," Perlstein calls it. Hearing it for the first time in his command trailer outside the hall, "White was so disgusted with what he could see only as a political disaster that he switched off his television monitor in rage."

There was a standing ovation in the hall. "Richard Nixon, making a snap political judgment, reached over to keep wife Pat in her seat. He was sick to his stomach." Scranton "glowered." A Goldwater man telling Romney he hoped the party would unite for victory "got back nothing but a bitter stare."

Next morning White learned from somebody who had heard it from somebody else that he was being removed from command of the campaign. The job went instead to Dean Burch, an Arizona liability lawyer whose only political qualification was friendship with the candidate. "Like a man on his deathbed," Perlstein writes, Goldwater "wanted to be surrounded only by friends." The Arizona amateurs were now in charge.

There were other factors that made a Johnson triumph nearly certain. The country was less than a year removed from the Kennedy assassination and only two years from the Cuban missile crisis and its close brush with nuclear war. The public was in no mood for the new excitements that would come with installing yet another president. Moreover, Johnson had done a masterful job of managing the transition after Kennedy's murder. With astonishing skill and speed, he had got through Congress a domestic program more ambitiously liberal than that of any president since Franklin Roosevelt. He cleverly exploited Goldwater's talk about atomic bombs, extremism, and tougher policies toward communism to paint Goldwater as a wild man.

For the first time in a long career Johnson found himself a beloved political figure. Until now his reputation had been that of a slick Texas wheeler-dealer, but that fall the public took to him with astonishing enthusiasm:

> People's response to seeing Johnson in the flesh was primal. Sometimes security men used their fists to keep crowds from smothering the President; sometimes they had to reach for their guns when rope lines snapped. Everywhere it was the same: people packed shoulder to shoulder as far as the eye could see. The President stood on his limousine seat and seemed to float above the crowd....
>
> In the spectacle liberal intellectuals spied Newtonian perfection: the pull toward consensus, the push away from extremism, a system regressing toward a safe, steady equilibrium.... Their young ruler had died, and they reached out to the new one with

raw, naked need, to fill an empty place, as if with his touch he could, just as he promised, *let us continue*, as if the bad things hadn't happened at all.

He was reelected with the biggest percentage of the vote ever. It was a triumph as exhilarating as Goldwater's had been at San Francisco, and, as with Goldwater, it was the father of disaster.

With the election won, Johnson waded deeper than ever before into the Vietnam War. Later the Pentagon Papers revealed that the administration had been planning all along to intensify the war. All along, while Johnson was declaring himself the peacemaker, plans for expanding the war were secretly being prepared. Exultant in political victory, Johnson proceeded to bomb, then to send more soldiers, then... Four years later his ruin was so complete that he surrendered the White House without trying to win a second term.

2.

Did the 1964 campaign really start something epochal? Perlstein says it "lit the fire that consumed an entire ideological universe, and made the opening years of the twenty-first century as surely a conservative epoch as the era between the New Deal and the Great Society was a liberal one." Recent political history suggests something a bit less cosmic has happened.

True, we are now governed by history's first court-appointed administration, thanks to five justices of the Supreme Court who are indeed conservatives, and the beneficiary of their intervention calls himself a "compassionate conservative." For the rest, though, conservatism has not run very well lately when put to the vote. Compassionately conservative Bush finished second behind Gore in the national popular vote. Conservatives lost control of the Senate, and the Republican majority in the House of Representatives was reduced to a wisp.

Conservatism itself seems to have turned into something quite different from the conservatism of 1964. The Supreme Court's taking charge of the presidential election in December of 2000 was a spectacular example of what conservatives of the Goldwater era used to deplore as judicial activism, a supposedly liberal vice.

Here is another eerie development: conservatism, which in Goldwater's day was unshakably committed to balancing the budget and reducing the national debt, managed to outdo two generations of liberal big spenders by quadrupling the debt during the twelve years of Reagan and Bush the Elder. And now we have the conservative younger Bush making a Keynesian argument for cutting taxes. In Goldwater's day conservatives regarded John Maynard Keynes's economic theories as only slightly less seditious than Karl Marx's.

One could go on listing strange mutations in conservatism since Goldwater—the rise of the clergyman as political boss, for instance, as with the Reverends Robertson and Falwell. What all this illustrates is the futility of discussing ideology with today's shopworn vocabulary. Words like "conservative" and "liberal" now mean whatever anybody saying or writing them wants them to mean. Wasn't it a Supreme Court justice who said he couldn't define pornography, but he knew what it was when he saw it? "Conservative" and "liberal" are like that. Where Perlstein sees the present political environment as a "conservative" epoch, it can be just as easily argued that an electorate unable to choose between Bush and Gore, far from blazing an ideological trail to the right, is drifting tranquilly toward slumber.

For most of the twentieth century American politics adhered to centrist ideas. Occasionally, as during the Depression, the country moved decidedly left; occasionally, as during the 1980s, decidedly right. The center, however, was traditionally the ground to seize and hold for politicians who wanted to win. By the time Clinton was elected the center had drifted rightward, and Clinton acknowledged this. Dukakis and Mondale had not, and had lost two presidential elections. Clinton may have won only because Ross Perot split the Republican vote in 1992, but once in office he acted on the assumption that the country had run out of enthusiasm for doing good and wanted to taste the pleasures of doing well.

Nudging Democrats off their traditional left-of-center ground, he moved them into the vacant trenches formerly occupied by "moderate" Republicans, a nearly extinct species, thanks to the conservatives' efforts to purge the party of impure ideas. There, dug in slightly to the right of the late Nelson Rockefeller, Democrats rediscovered the rewards that normally accrue to American politicians holding the middle of the road. They might be enjoying them still but for the importunate Monica Lewinsky and Gore's curious inability to find out who he was.

The middle of the road was where both parties had traditionally thrived while fighting over the distinctions between tittles and jots. In America the middle ruled. People who moved out of it, leftward or right, were deplored and scolded as "extremists"—deplored because leaving the middle led so often to defeat, scolded because extremism had been made to seem radical and un-American. That was the burden of Johnson's attack on Goldwater: he was an extremist and extremists were bad.

Senator Robert A. Taft, conservatism's tragic hero, had argued against the centrist consensus long before Goldwater's time. Taft believed there was a big conservative vote which never went to the polls because Republicans never chose a truly conservative presidential candidate. William Buckley, with his gift for blood-stirring prose, turned Taft's argument into a challenge to combat: "Middle-of-the-road...is politically, intellectually, and morally repugnant."

Perlstein's subtitle, "Barry Goldwater and the Unmaking of the American Consensus," alludes to the Republican departure from middle-of-the-road politics in 1964. He is not persuasive, though, in arguing that this ended the consensus. To be sure, signs of new life appeared soon after the defeat, and the word "conservatism" lost its stigma. Candidates began calling themselves "conservatives" and winning lesser elections, and sometimes bigger elections. Ronald Reagan became governor of California.

Yet the sixteen years between Goldwater's defeat and the start of Reagan's presidency produced no notable reversal of the "big government" domestic policies rooted in the New Deal. In those years Johnson, Nixon, Ford, and Carter continued strengthening the welfare state. By the time Reagan arrived it had become such an entrenched part of American life that the Reagan people trying to root it out thought of themselves as revolutionaries, rather than conservatives. Conservatives are supposed to preserve tradition, not destroy it. They might have more correctly called themselves reactionaries for they were people unresigned to long tradition and were fighting to destroy a political culture their parents and grandparents had hated since Peter Arno cartooned them in 1936 going to a newsreel theater "to hiss Roosevelt."

Reagan himself was anything but reactionary. He had firmly held ideas about changes he wanted in foreign and economic policy. Dismantling the welfare state was not a high priority. He cautiously avoided assaults on Social Security and health care programs. While talking eloquently about the importance of school prayer and the rights of the unborn, he did nothing of consequence to restore classroom praying or end abortion, possibly because his polls showed these were losing issues.

And so the right's glorious Reagan years ended with some of its most passionately held goals still unreached. The right was uneasy about the succession of the elder Bush. Conservatives were people of sunny southlands, and though he claimed to like pork rinds, Bush came from the same Northeastern, Ivy League, internationalist, Wall

Street crowd that had sulked on the sidelines while Goldwater was being humiliated by Johnson. Worse than that, he had raised taxes!

If the senior Bush was hard for conservatives to suffer, Bill Clinton drove them near to madness. The history of their attempts to destroy Clinton and their constant failures to do so is a garish tale of politics as pathology. Clinton's ability to defeat them time and again while governing in accord with the hated old moderate-Republican reliance on consensus mocked the notion that conservatism had won a great ideological victory. Clinton demonstrated that consensus remained as powerful as it had been before Goldwater.

If ever an epoch of conservatism seemed at hand, it was when the 1994 elections gave Newt Gingrich command of the House of Representatives. The moment was brief. Gingrich attempted a conservative putsch against Clinton, Clinton emerged triumphant, and Gingrich disappeared from public life. Encouraged by the sex scandals, conservatives tried impeaching Clinton. Without the votes to convict him in the Senate, they succeeded only in producing an unusually high public-approval rating for his presidential performance. The public did not like his vulgar sexual behavior, but it clearly liked government by centrist consensus more than government by an angry right.

3.

Modern conservatism owes much of its success to the aggressive political activity of evangelical Christian churches. In Goldwater's era they stayed out of politics; now they crack whips. When young Bush needed a primary-election victory over John McCain in South Carolina in 2000, he did his duty to the church by speaking at Bob Jones University, famous as an intellectual citadel of the racially segregated life. McCain, realizing that the Christian right was about to do him in, lost his temper, spoke angrily about the tactics of certain political churchmen, and so assured Bush of a big victory.

This was a far different conservatism from Goldwater's 1964 variety. Like Calvin Coolidge, Goldwater believed that the business of America was business. Today's conservatism, heavily influenced by a Christian fundamentalist vote, holds that the business of America is also morality. The result is a politics passionately devoted to argument about family life, abortion, religion, and sex.

The history of the evangelical entry into politics is fascinating and complicated. There is an excellent account in *Right-Wing Populism in America*, by Chip Berlet and Matthew N. Lyons, whose book describes the outermost fringes of American conservatism.[3] The story involves the Book of Revelations, Satan, the Antichrist, the End Times—a period of widespread sinfulness, moral depravity, and crass materialism—and disagreement among Premillennialists about whether faithful Christians will experience no Tribulations, some Tribulations, or all Tribulations. The history of how all this led these austere Protestants to enter the house of conservatism is intricate, absorbing, and worth studying by everyone who enjoys sounding off against the Christian fundamentalists and wishes he knew something about them.

Equally important to conservative success has been the disappearance of the white Democratic vote in the South. This began with the passage of the 1964 Civil Rights Bill. Johnson, who masterminded its enactment, said at the time it would be the end of his party in the South. To his credit he signed it anyhow and proved himself an accurate prophet. White Southern Democrats vanished fast, some because they tried to remain Democrats, others because they quickly underwent party-change surgery and turned into Republicans. This gave us today's Dixieland version of the party of Lincoln as the party of Trent Lott and Tom DeLay.

---

3. *Right-Wing Populism in America: Too Close for Comfort* (Guilford Press, 2000).

It would be silly to pretend that racism is not a factor here. Racism has always been the unmentionable guest at conservatism's table. Conservatives insist it is principle, not bigotry, that compels them to oppose civil rights bills, affirmative action, and all such soft-hearted and fuzzy-minded attempts to equalize the distribution of America's boons. Whatever the explanation, the South that had been solidly Democratic so long as Democratic presidents let Jim Crow flourish became solidly Republican after Democrats became identified with civil rights causes.

Goldwater would doubtless have embarrassed today's conservatives. He had never liked mixing religion in politics and thought government had no business legislating on moral issues. When he was eighty-five and long out of politics, he lent his name to gay rights activities and spoke out on behalf of gays in the military. One of his grandsons was homosexual. People have a constitutional right to be homosexual, he told the *Washington Post* reporter Lloyd Grove. He had just backed a Democrat running for Congress against a Christian conservative, and he spoke tartly of "fellows like Pat Robertson...trying to take the Republican Party away from the Republican Party, and make a religious organization out of it. If that ever happens, kiss politics goodbye."

He was still the model of indiscreet speech, still speaking his mind on the late Lyndon Johnson, "the most dishonest man we ever had in the Presidency," he told Grove. In his autobiography he had called Johnson "the epitome of the unprincipled politician," "a dirty fighter," a man who would "slap you on the back today and stab you in the back tomorrow." The only other politician he detested as heartily was Richard Nixon: "a two-fisted, four-square liar," he wrote.

Chapter 10

CRUEL AND USUAL

1.

THE DEATH PENALTY was already falling into disuse in the United States when the Supreme Court ended it in 1972. There had been no executions for five years. Death houses were still filled with candidates, but the old zest for sending convicts to the gallows, the chair, and the gas chamber seemed to have waned. State governors, whose duties include the macabre obligation to sign death warrants, were increasingly finding reasons to commute capital sentences to life imprisonment or to grant extended delays of execution. What Justice Harry Blackmun called the "machinery of death" had come to a slow idle.

Then something happened. By the middle of the 1970s there was a rising public clamor for capital punishment. Politicians were discovering that pledges to be "tough on crime" worked like catnip on voters, and who could be "tougher" than the candidate howling for the death penalty? Mr. Dooley was not joking when he said the Supreme Court follows the election returns; by 1976 it had decided that capital punishment was not "cruel and unusual" after all; executioners came back to work.

Nowadays American devotion to capital punishment is such that only the most foolhardy governor would dare confess that signing a death warrant doesn't make him sleep better. Periodically congressmen call attention to their "toughness" by discovering more federal crimes that require capital punishment. Periodically politicians denounce the entire legal system for making it hard to clear out the death houses with dispatch. Recently a Missouri man nominated for a federal judgeship was blocked by his state's Republican senator, John Ashcroft, because of a "poor record on the death penalty."

William S. McFeely, the biographer of Frederick Douglass and General Grant, found himself performing in this Grand Guignol when he was asked to testify in the Georgia sentencing trial of a man convicted of kidnapping, rape, and murder. A distinguished historian, Profesor McFeely had been opposed to the death penalty on philosophical grounds, but "proximity" to a man very likely to die in the electric chair seems to have produced an emotional loathing for it.

His short book, *Proximity to Death*,* is a tribute to the Southern Center for Human Rights, a small band of lawyers based in Atlanta, and especially to Stephen Bright, who is not their leader but the "first among equals." Their goal is to save clients from "the ultimate expression of violence," which, in McFeely's phrase, is "the state killing its own people." Because of work like theirs, years often elapse nowadays before a court's sentence of death is carried out. The average time between conviction and execution in Georgia is over eight years. One of the center's clients whom McFeely met was still in prison eighteen years after being sentenced, and his case still in court on appeal.

Bright and his colleagues are people whom the steamier proponents of capital punishment love to hate: lawyers who use what Senator Orrin Hatch calls "frivolous appeals" to impede swift exaction of the state's "awful vengeance." Why do they do it? Not for money. No one in the group is paid more than $23,000 a year. And few jobs can be grimmer; this one often ends with a lawyer attending his client's execution.

---

*Norton, 2000.

McFeely finds the answer in a courtroom confrontation between Stephen Bright, arguing for the life of one Carzell Moore, and Tommy K. Floyd, a district attorney, arguing for Moore's execution:

> They stand as exemplars of two fundamentally different philosophical positions on the death penalty. Bright and Floyd guard gates—of different cities.
>
> Carzell Moore has been convicted for an act so terrible that neither guardian would lightly allow this man the freedom of his city's streets. One, to sustain the city, would use the law's authority to banish from life a being no longer within his concept of human; the other would claim that no person is ever wholly outside the city's wall. Though Moore has raped and murdered—has sacked his own city—he is, to Stephen Bright, still of its people. For the authorities of that city, for its citizens, to match his act of killing with a killing, to deny even him life, is for the city to lose its very civility.

Here is the debate in its classic terms: Is the death penalty essential to preserve a civilized society, or is it a relic of barbarity mocking society's claim to be civilized? Bright's group acts on the principle that no crime, no matter how monstrous, can justify a civilized people in killing its perpetrator. It is a lonely position these days. McFeely concludes that Justice Antonin Scalia came closer to speaking the popular mind when he "forthrightly advocated retribution as a proper motivation for the death penalty."

This enthusiasm for capital punishment is not easily explained. It flourishes at a moment when most other industrial nations have turned against it. Today it is either abolished or in disuse throughout Western Europe, in most of the former Eastern European Communist bloc countries, and in Russia. Israel, since its founding, has used it only once, with the hanging of Adolf Eichmann. The modern industrial world seems to have abandoned it out of some embarrassed sense that it is a barbaric vestige of an archaic culture. Professor McFeely is hard pressed to explain why the United States, "with its claim to moral leadership of the world," has gone in precisely the opposite direction. Our "vigorous use of the death penalty," he notes, puts us "in company with Iran, Iraq, the United Arab Emirates, and Yemen." Writing in 2002, he would surely have added China.

He examines several theories about why Americans are now so fond of it. One holds that the United States is so singularly infested with criminals that an exasperated public demands Draconian measures for self-protection. This appetite is whetted by local television news shows saturated with crime stories and by the spectacular nature of terrorist crimes like the bombings of Oklahoma City's federal office building and New York's World Trade Center.

There is great political mileage to be had from exploiting these public passions; hence the politicians' incessant campaign promises to be "tough on crime." And so when elected they vote for ever "tougher" punishments: long-term imprisonment for minor drug offenders, life sentences for bad apples with several felony convictions, and application of the death penalty to a wider variety of crimes.

The underlying assumption of this theory is that a testy public must be humored by aggressive use of the death penalty. The problem with this is that the theory presumes a degree of brutality in the public spirit that seems inconsistent with the present increase in America's Christian churchgoing population. Puzzling about this contradiction, McFeely wanders into the theological bogs, borrowing from a theory about lynchings which was formulated by Donald D. Matthews, a historian of American religion. Why, Matthews wondered, had religion and lynching "waxed" simultaneously in the South of the 1890s? Perhaps it was because the Christianity then popular in the South devalued a compassionate New Testament God in favor of the "stern and inscrutable God of Israel." Christ had to suffer death on the cross to provide atonement for the original sin of which all humanity was guilty. Thus, "at the heart of salvation," Matthews writes, "were the metaphors of retributive justice: at the center was a symbol of torture and death."

Then, McFeely: "So imbued with this belief system were some adherents of lynching—and now executions—that for them, only with a killing can we atone for the sins of the society or one of its worst miscreants." This may be a theory that only a theologian can love, but at least it offers a pious rationale for what many now consider an unholy policy.

Other theories are more profane. One argues that the enthusiasm for executions expresses the hardiness of undying American racism, for a high proportion of the condemned are black. Another suggests it is part of the conservative reaction against the tolerant culture of the late Sixties and early Seventies. Many a small-bore Jeremiah now blames those years for creating such rot in the nation's moral code that our very survival is at risk. Which brings us back again to the old dispute about who holds the high moral ground in this endless debate.

When he was solicitor general arguing before the Supreme Court for restoration of the death penalty, Robert Bork said the state could legitimately "conclude that capital punishment serves a vital social function as society's expression of moral outrage." A "venting of outrage at the violation of society's most important rules," he argued, "is itself an important, perhaps a necessary, social function...." McFeely prefers the opposed view of what is moral, represented by Justice Thurgood Marshall, who held that it was the death penalty itself that violated society's rules.

The ascendancy of the New Democrats under Bill Clinton cannot be ignored. This group realized that Democrats had to combat the Republicans' claim to be the "tough-on-crime" party by matching them in "toughness." To illustrate that he was leading a "tough-on-crime" party, candidate Clinton interrupted his 1992 campaign, returned to Little Rock, and did his gubernatorial duty by signing a death warrant for a mentally defective man.

Democratic Governor Bob Graham of Florida was put to the test by the sentencing of John Spenkelink, the first man condemned in Florida after the Supreme Court restored capital punishment in 1976. McFeely describes immense pressure on Graham to be merciful. He had once been opposed to the death penalty.

> Though said to be agonizing over a grant of clemency, the governor, as one of the new breed of southern Democrats with reconstructed racial views, thought it essential to balance that stance with a toughness on crime. To hold him fast to that resolve, Graham's fellow young governor, Bill Clinton of Arkansas, called with legal advice, lest Graham make a mistake and jeopardize the restoration of the death penalty in other states.

Spenkelink was electrocuted, and Florida now stands with Texas and Virginia among states most likely to apply the penalty.

2.

For all the fervor among death-penalty adherents, they are curiously squeamish about how the thing is to be done. The 2000 session of the Supreme Court agreed to consider whether Florida's notoriously troublesome electric chair was exacting "cruel and unusual" punishment with performances *The New York Times* delicately called "messy." No one expected the present Court to enlarge the case by considering whether execution itself amounts to cruel and unusual punishment, and the question became moot when Florida abandoned its chair and shifted to death by lethal injection. Putting people to death was not the issue; the issue was how to put them to death neatly.

This is a matter that has troubled societies throughout history. The Roman historian Livy, writing during the golden Augustan Age, was still appalled by the way one Mettius Fufetius had been executed six-and-a-half centuries earlier, about 670 BC. Mettius was tied, spread-eagled, between two chariots, each drawn by four horses. "At a touch of the whip the two teams sprang forward in opposite directions, carrying with them the fragments of the mangled body still held by the ropes. All eyes were averted from the disgusting spectacle."

This technique obviously offends Livy's Roman pride. He seems to think it so revolting that Romans will be ashamed to read of it, for he hastens to reassure them:

> That was the first and last time that fellow-countrymen of ours inflicted a punishment so utterly without regard to the laws of humanity. Save for that one instance we can fairly claim to have been content with more humane forms of punishment than any other nation.

Well, this may be doubtful, but how modern of him to disapprove of "messy" executions. Like our Supreme Court pondering Florida's electric chair, he is concerned not with morality but with technology.

Many cultures have exulted in the messiness with which executions could be done and tried to make them ever more dreadful, as though the death agony should match the gravity of the crime. In England during Tudor and Stuart times, people guilty of treason might be publicly hanged, drawn, and quartered. Condemned people of high breeding might be let off with a private beheading in the Tower of London.

Dreadful public executions were doubtless intended to deter crime by showing the masses how unpleasant its consequences could be, but the public seems to have flocked to them more for thrills than for edification. The tireless seducer Giovanni Giacomo Casanova tells of a woman looking down from an open window who allowed him to have his way with her while she watched an especially nasty execution in a public square.

Within the present century, hangings in America were often conducted in a circus atmosphere. In his days as a police reporter, H. L. Mencken attended an assortment of them in Maryland's county jailhouse yards. His first, in 1899, was "a hanging of the very first chop" since four men were to be "stretched at once." Several witnesses and reporters were "wobbling" drunk before the event began, and a half-dozen "fell in swoons, and had to be evacuated by the cops." On one occasion, Mencken reports, a giant of a man

> fought Joe [the hangman] and the sheriff on the scaffold, knocked out the county cops who came to their aid, leaped down into the bellowing crowd, broke out of the jail yard, and took to an adjacent forest. It was an hour or more before he was run down and brought back. By that time all the fight had oozed out of him, and Joe and the sheriff turned him off with quiet elegance.

By 1947, when I came to Maryland journalism, the era of circus at the scaffold had ended, though I met a few old cops who talked nostalgically of it. The trend in execution was toward something that might be loosely called dignity, although in Maryland it also seemed that everybody thought something shameful was being done. The hangings were done at midnight in a small white-walled brick chamber at the state penitentiary in Baltimore. The atmosphere was unrelievedly grim. The number of witnesses was limited and whiskey forbidden. I had the good fortune never to attend one. A newspaper colleague relieved me of the assignment. He saw three men dropped through the trap and was sick for days.

Nowadays it is common for demonstrators to gather outside the prison as a convict's final hours are counted down. This produces the only remnant of the theater of execution that once titillated crowds and gave the condemned a chance, perhaps for the first time in his life, to address a large audience. Professor McFeely conveys the mood of these modern demonstrations, using testimony about Georgia's execution of Roosevelt Green.

The demonstration area was divided into sections, one for the press, one for Ku Klux Klan members, and one for people opposing the death penalty. Klan members wore traditional robes and held signs. The witness recalls that "most of the signs were jingles that said something like, 'Now he's going to burn, now he's going to fry, now he's going to shake, now he's going to die,' that sort of thing." Their mood was "angry, hostile, and eventually celebrative."

Another witness had brought his wife and teenage children for the occasion. He remembered "some celebrating" after the crowd heard the execution had taken place. "When they brought the hearse out, I remember the crowd jumping up and down and celebrating."

Edward Stephens, a former Grand Dragon of the Georgia Klan, didn't remember Green's execution "standing out over and above the other seven or eight executions that I've went down there in support of the death penalty on...."

Stephens's reaction to news of any execution was "joyful relief that it's another burden off the taxpayer's back." Opponents of the death penalty, he went on, "stand around and hold candles and cry because a person has just been executed. But they don't think anything of the victims. We rejoice that the person that has created the crime, that has taken a person's life and extinguished it like a cigarette butt has been put to rest, and hopefully sent to where's he's supposed to be, no matter what color he is."

Chapter 11

OUT OF STEP WITH THE WORLD

1.

JOSEPH MITCHELL'S New York is long vanished. We can only argue about whose New York has succeeded it, but Tom Wolfe's, painted in his broad, gaudy burlesque strokes, would have to be considered. With its lunatic obsession with money, New York from Reagan through Giuliani has become too grotesque to be captured by mere satire. Satire is subtle; turn-of-the-millennium New York runs irresistibly to grossness.

In *The Bonfire of the Vanities* Wolfe has a character die while dining in a fancy East Side restaurant and paints a scene, both hilarious and disgusting, in which the management's only concerns are to get the body out fast and to collect the bill for the dead man's unfinished meal. They end up shoving the body through a toilet window. It is hard to recall a more savage literary comment on New York's character.

Some readers thought Wolfe unjustly cruel to the city, and maybe he was. Still, in the present New York people go out to dinner, pay a thousand dollars a bottle for the wine, and go home to three-million-dollar apartments while others are bedding down on sidewalks in cardboard boxes. Only burlesque can catch the spirit of it.

New Yorks come and go so quickly that literature has trouble keeping up with them. From Washington Irving to Poe to Melville to

Whitman to Edith Wharton, somebody's "old New York" has always been turning into a new city. Joseph Mitchell became its chronicler as F. Scott Fitzgerald was leaving the scene, and Mitchell's city would have absolutely none of the gauzy romantic charm of Fitzgerald's. Fitzgerald's New York was a 1920 prairie boy's dream of white towers and gloriously desirable girls, but Daisy Buchanan already belonged to a past as remote as Lillian Russell and Boss Tweed on the day Mitchell arrived in town. That was October 25, 1929. The stock market had crashed the day before.

Mitchell was not much for romantic charm anyhow, but in a dark time he saw and painted the city as a place with a great sweetness of character which eased the hard lives he recorded. His New York was born of the crash, hardened by the Great Depression, civilized by the sense of mission generated by World War II, and made genial by the Eisenhower era's sense of well-being.

When he stopped writing in the 1960s the inevitable change was almost complete. The martini hour was ending; marijuana, hallucinogens, and the needle in the arm were the new way. The tinkling piano in the next apartment was giving way to the guitar in the park. People now had so much money that they could afford to look poor. Men quit wearing fedoras and three-piece suits to Yankee Stadium and affected a hobo chic—all whiskers and no creases. Women quit buying hats and high-heeled shoes and started swearing like Marine sergeants. College students, who had once rioted for the pure joy of it, began rioting for moral and political uplift, issued non-negotiable demands, held the dean hostage, and blew up the physics lab. Gangster funerals disappeared into the back of the newspapers, upstaged by spectacular nationally televised funerals of murdered statesmen.

Mitchell stopped writing, but through the middle third of the twentieth century he had created a tapestry of New York lives comparable to Charles Dickens's astonishing assortment of Victorian Londoners. To be sure, Dickens's most memorable people were fictional while Mitchell's had all actually lived and breathed, but just as Dickens's fictional Londoners seem more real than life, Mitchell's real New Yorkers seem born to live in novels.

In *McSorley's Wonderful Saloon*,[1] he produces Charles Eugene Cassell, who operates Captain Charley's Private Museum for Intelligent People in a Fifty-ninth Street basement, admission fifteen cents when he remembers to collect it. Captain Charley brings to mind Dickens's Mr. Venus, the taxidermist in *Our Mutual Friend*, who has acquired the rascally Silas Wegg's amputated leg bone. Mitchell reports visiting the museum one day to find the Captain "searching for a bone which he said he hacked off an Arab around 9 PM one full-moon night in 1907 after the Arab had been murdered for signing a treaty...."

Like Dickens, Mitchell roamed his city looking for people worth preserving in stories. Dickens found the makings of Sairy Gamp, Mister Bumble, and Gaffer Hexam, who fished the Thames for corpses of men who might have drowned with money in their pockets. Mitchell found Cockeye Johnny, one of New York's several gypsy "kings," and through him learned of the superior cunning of gypsy women and how to operate a classic swindle the gypsies called "bajour"; Commodore Dutch, who for forty years made his living by giving an annual ball for the benefit of himself; and Arthur Samuel Colborne, founder of the Anti-Profanity League, who devoted his life to stamping out cussing in New York, or, as Colborne put it, "cleaning up profanity conditions."

> I'm past seventy, but I'm a go-getter, fighting the evil on all fronts. Keeps me busy. I'm just after seeing a high official at City Hall. There's some Broadway plays so profane it's a wonder to me the tongues of the actors and the actresses don't wither up and come loose at the roots and drop to the ground, and I

---

1. Pantheon, 2001.

beseeched this high official to take action. Said he'd do what he could. Probably won't do a single, solitary thing.

It won't do to press the Dickens parallel too hard. Mitchell himself doesn't seem to have been especially interested in Dickens. His favorite writers were Mark Twain and James Joyce. His passion for Joyce ran so deep that he guessed he'd read *Finnegans Wake* a half-dozen times. Moreover, though Dickens and Mitchell both began as reporters fascinated by the dark side of city life, Dickens was a deep-dyed moralizer whose journalistic style would have horrified Mitchell. In *The Uncommercial Traveler*, a book of reporting, Dickens visits a London workhouse, views the bleak lives of the aged, sick, addled, and orphaned who are stored in such places in 1850, and writes:

> In ten minutes I had ceased to believe in such fables of a golden time as youth, the prime of life, or a hale old age. In ten minutes, all the lights of womankind seemed to have been blown out, and nothing in that way to be left this vault to brag of, but the flickering and expiring snuffs.

This is classic Dickens on an emotional binge, and it would have appalled Mitchell. Dickens's inability to keep his passions out of his writing may have helped make him a great novelist, but it made for some very bad journalism. Mitchell, whose few attempts at fiction were not notably successful, was incapable of sermonizing about the hardships of his subjects. Serious reporters were not supposed to do that, and he thought of himself as a reporter, not a man of letters. He was trained in the hard discipline of an old-fashioned journalism whose code demanded self-effacement of the writer. A reporter's effusions about his own inner turmoil were taboo.

The discipline by which he worked required something like the artistry needed to compose good music: the writer had to stir an emotional or intellectual response in his audience without telling them how to feel or think. The portraits of people who caught his fancy are worth close study by writers who want to learn how to move an audience without preaching a lesson. These pieces usually start as if they are going to be funny, then almost deliberately deceive this expectation and become touching and sometimes terribly sad, as in "Lady Olga."

Here his subject is Jane Barnell, a sixty-nine-year-old woman whose life has been spent as a "bearded lady" in circus sideshows. She has a thick, curly, gray beard thirteen-and-a-half inches long and is working in the basement sideshow of Hubert's Museum on Forty-second Street when Mitchell meets her in 1940. She has recently left Ringling Brothers and Barnum & Bailey because union trouble ended its season and is afraid that if she goes back "that union will get me." A "violently opinionated Republican," though she never votes, she believes everything she reads in the Hearst newspapers and assumes "the average union organizer carries a gun and will shoot to kill."

But Mitchell is not dwelling on her "freakishness" to provide the reader with a supercilious smile. He is out to explore what it means to be a "freak" in America, and the notion that we are going to be titillated with anecdotes about Miss Barnell's bizarre appearance vanishes as he piles up details. What emerges is a portrait of a woman who has spent most of her life in pain:

> In an expansive mood, she will brag that she has the longest female beard in history and will give the impression that she feels superior to less spectacular women. Every so often, however, hurt by a snicker or a brutal remark made by someone in an audience, she undergoes a period of depression that may last a few hours or a week. "When I get the blues, I feel like an outcast from society," she once said. "I used to think when I got old my feelings wouldn't get hurt, but I was wrong. I got a tougher hide than I once had, but it ain't tough enough."

Because Miss Barnell's sideshow colleagues were touchy about the word "freak," the Ringling circus—in a prehistoric concession to political correctness—changed the name of its Congress of Freaks to Congress of Strange People. Miss Barnell cannot cheer. "No matter how nice a name was put on me," she tells Mitchell, "I would still have a beard." Considering herself engaged in show business as truly as any Broadway actor, she holds that "a freak is just as good as any actor, from the Barrymores on down." Mitchell lets her speak the closing line of his story, perhaps because it speaks the message he would speak himself if he felt free to preach as Dickens did: "'If the truth was known, we're all freaks together,' she says."

2.

Although Mitchell wrote voluminously about the kind of people the world happily ignored until he wrote about them, he wrote very little about himself. My *Ears Are Bent*, written in 1938, was his only extended exercise in self-advertisement. It is a small, modest book about his early newspaper days with the *Herald Tribune* and the *World-Telegram*. Published when he was thirty, it was out of print for decades, but is now back in the shops in a new, slightly refreshed edition.[2]

This is not the mature, polished work of the later *New Yorker* pieces, but the writing is already remarkable for its economy, precision, and power to get at what makes odd people more interesting than their oddness. From the very beginning he seems to have had a perfect ear for the astonishing quotation; he cannot resist telling of the streetwalker who, asked why she had become a prostitute, replied, "I just wanted to be accommodating."

---

2. Pantheon, 2001.

The people he liked writing about as a young reporter foreshadowed the kind of people who later filled his long *New Yorker* profiles, all of which are now collected in the 1992 *Up in the Old Hotel*[3] and the new reissue of *McSorley's Wonderful Saloon*. They were people who were "sadly or humorously out of step with the world," as Brendan Gill described them. Mitchell found them in places to which middle-class New Yorkers paid little attention: the Bowery, the waterfront, the fish market, Times Square corners where preachers harangued passing sinners, and workingmen's saloons where bartenders were gentle when tossing out a panhandler.

It was usually said that his subjects were "eccentrics." This is journalistic lingo for people who are notably different from the run-of-the-mine population but neither successful nor rich enough to merit journalistic attention. Mitchell seemed to reason that, regardless of being unsuccessful or poor, eccentricity might make them more interesting than the run-of-the-mine majority, and he cultivated them from his early newspaper days. When the news was slow they might provide a small human-interest feature.

Among the specimens he found was a man named Reidt who was obsessed with predicting the end of the world—"always going up on a hilltop...with his family to await destruction." The Reidt connection finally paid off one dull news day when Mitchell "called him up to ask if he had any advance information on the crack of doom and the telephone operator said, 'Mr. Reidt's telephone has been disconnected.'"

A reporter writing features in New York papers also met eccentrics who were successful and well-heeled. He sketched a few in this early book. George Bernard Shaw is here. Huey Long sits in bed with a hangover at the Waldorf-Astoria, wearing baby-blue pajamas, scratching his toes, and telling a long incoherent story about a relative who

---

3. Vintage, 1992.

owned a saloon. Billy Sunday, the old baseball player turned evangelist ("Hit a home run for Jesus!"), is interviewed in bed too at his hotel, wearing woolen winter underwear, scratching his itching back, and husbanding his strength for the night's revival meeting. ("I wanted to take me a walk around town ... but Ma made me get in bed and take a nap.") He takes a ride with Mary Louise Cecilia (Texas) Guinan in her bullet-proof limousine, talks about her playing the role of Aimee Semple McPherson on Broadway, suggests that Mrs. McPherson would surely sue the producer, and faithfully records Miss Guinan's response. ("'That,' said Miss Guinan, 'is no skin off my ass.'")

Most of those mentioned here were more interesting than famous. Among them is Florence Cubitt, sitting in an overstuffed hotel room chair wearing only a G-string and "a cheerful baby face," the only garb appropriate when "Tanya, Queen of the Nudists" submits to an interview. To promote her career she has taken the name Tanya in the belief that "Tanya sounds more sexy than Florence." She has been performing at a trade fair in San Diego and is in town with a press agent to stir up demand for including a nude show at the coming New York World's Fair of 1939. She explains that in the San Diego show twenty young women and five men played games in the nude on a big field while customers (admission forty cents) watched from a distance.

"The men nudists are a bunch of nuts," she tells Mitchell. "Why, they eat peas right out of the pod. They squeeze the juice out of vegetables and drink it, and they don't eat salt. Also, they have long beards. They don't have any ambition. They just want to be nudists all their lives." Then, in her tribute to the nudist life, Mitchell catches a glimpse of innocence too unspoiled to be believed:

> "It keeps us out in the open," said Miss Cubitt. "It doesn't keep us out late at night, and we have a healthy atmosphere to work in. My girl friends think we have orgies and all, but I never had an orgy yet. Sometimes when the sun is hot, nudism is hard work."

This early book is a rare instance of Mitchell writing—at least a little—about himself. By the end of the very first page he has told us he comes from North Carolina, attended the university at Chapel Hill, left it (doesn't say why), and while recuperating from an appendectomy read James Bryce's *American Commonwealth*, which made him want to become a political reporter, so came to New York at the age of twenty-one "with that idea in mind."

This is surely the most modest newspaper reporter since Gutenberg first inked a press: not a word about his family history, his childhood, his educational travails, his youthful loves and hates, his early triumphs and humiliations, how he started writing, why he decided to come to New York, or how a self-effacing youngster from the sticks was able to land a job on the elegant *Herald Tribune*.

The *Tribune* sent him up to Harlem to cover police stories, and he found himself sitting in a swivel chair in the doorway of the Theresa Hotel watching the passing parade on Seventh Avenue. In Harlem he found his calling, and it was not political reporting. Harlem fascinated him. He had grown up white in the South during a stifling and benighted racist era, and the freedom he found in Harlem seems to have been exhilarating:

> I was alternately delighted and frightened out of my wits by what I saw at night in Harlem. I would go off duty at 3 AM, and then I would walk around the streets and look, discovering what the depression and the prurience of white men were doing to a people who are "last to be hired; first to be fired."

He might "drop into a speakeasy or a night club or a gambling flat and try to pull a story out of it. I got to know a few underworld figures and I used to like to listen to them talk."

His *New Yorker* stories are told in great rivers of talk to which Mitchell seems to have listened so intensely that the talker couldn't resist talking more, and more, and more. He had the gift of listening, but what made him special was his knack for finding people worth listening to. In *My Ears Are Bent*, he discussed how to find them:

> The only people I do not care to listen to are society women, industrial leaders, distinguished authors, ministers, explorers, moving picture actors (except W. C. Fields and Stepin Fetchit), and any actress under the age of thirty-five. I believe the most interesting human beings, so far as talk is concerned, are anthropologists, farmers, prostitutes, psychiatrists, and an occasional bartender. The best talk is artless, the talk of people trying to reassure or comfort themselves, women in the sun, grouped around baby carriages, talking about their weeks in the hospital or the way meat has gone up, or men in saloons, talking to combat the loneliness everyone feels.

3.

Mitchell, who died in 1996, published almost nothing during the final thirty years of his life. He did not announce that he was going out of business or retire to enjoy rustic solitude and ostentatiously refuse to grant interviews. He did not clean out his desk while mourning colleagues watched. He did not even stop coming to the office.

Only gradually was it observed that, while he came to the office as regularly as ever, he no longer submitted anything for publication. His office was at *The New Yorker*, a magazine then famous for not pressing writers to produce. Even in his prime Mitchell had been known there as a man who took his good old time with a story. "Excellent quality, low productivity," Harold Ross, the magazine's founder-editor said of him in 1946.

It worried people that he quit writing. American writers are conditioned by the nation's market culture to suppose that no amount of success can explain why a writer sound of mind and body should cease production after thirty or forty years of what, for most writers at least, is an extremely exacting and decidedly lonely line of work. When it happens the publishing world is troubled. Something psychologically alarming must have happened. People want an explanation.

Calvin Trillin, who knew Mitchell during the years of silence, treats the silence lightly in his foreword to *McSorley's Wonderful Saloon*:

> During the decades when Mitchell came to the offices of *The New Yorker* every day but never turned anything in, one of the many fanciful stories heard as an explanation for his silence was that he had been writing at the same pace as everyone else until some college professor said that he was the greatest master of the English declarative sentence in America, and that this encomium had stopped him cold.

This suggests that the fancies of Mitchell's colleagues tended toward the idea of "writer's block," a disease especially widespread among college students which leaves its victim's writing faculties in a state of paralysis, rendering him powerless to put words on paper for fear they may reveal he is not yet Shakespeare's equal. Since it is a disease of egocentrics (also of people who want to be famous writers but don't much like to write), Mitchell would have been immune; as a reporter he always left his ego at home when he went to work.

As for paralysis, there is evidence that in his eighties he could write as gracefully as he wrote at forty and fifty. When *Up in the Old Hotel* was published in 1992, Mitchell, then eighty-four, contributed an "Author's Note" remarkable for the beauty with which it evoked a sense of his childhood. Never before had he written so intimately about himself. It contained a hint that he had been amused by his colleagues' curiosity about the long silence. "I am sure that most of the influences responsible for one's cast of mind are too remote and mysterious to be known," he wrote, and then—in an extraordinary concession—went on to say, "but I happen to know a few of the influences responsible for mine."

And he wrote of summer Sundays in a Southern childhood.

Like so many who wrote so well about New York, he was an out-of-towner. He was born in 1908 into a well-to-do North Carolina farm family and raised in a small town misnamed Fairmont—"no *monts* in or around it or anywhere near it," he wrote. It was situated some sixty miles from the ocean in an area of flat, rich, black farmland intercut with swamp waters and piney woods. The family had grown cotton, tobacco, corn, and timber in that part of the world since before the Revolutionary War.

As in a lot of the rural South, families there commonly buried the dead in their farm fields, creating small private cemeteries shaded by groves of cedar or magnolia and enclosed by cast-iron fences. Generations of Mitchell kin were scattered among these small burying grounds, and they were not allowed to be forgotten quickly. On Sundays the family went for drives along country roads:

> Now and then my father would stop the car and we would get out and visit one of those cemeteries, and my father or mother would tell us gravestone by gravestone who the people were who were buried there and exactly how they were related to us. I always enjoyed those visits.

Summertime brought a traditional family watermelon-cutting ceremony in a picnic grove behind an old church his mother's ancestors had helped build. When the melons were eaten and family talk was winding down and the afternoon was getting late, his Aunt Annie would lead a procession into the cemetery talking about the past, now and then pausing at a grave to "tell us about the man or woman down below." Some of her memories were "horrifying," some "horrifyingly funny."

Here were the cultural odds and ends associated with the making of the "Southern writer": cemeteries and ancestors, family get-togethers behind the church Grandfather helped to build, Sunday drives down country roads. And those watermelons—in his eighties Mitchell could still see them, "pulled early that morning in our own gardens—long, heavy, green-striped Georgia Rattlesnakes and big, round, heavy Cuban Queens so green they were almost black."

Looking back at his work in old age, he was "surprised and pleased" to find it filled with what he thought was "graveyard humor." In some it was "what the story is all about," he said, and it pleased him that the work was so full of it because "graveyard humor is an exemplification of the way I look at the world."

It doesn't seem odd that he should have stopped writing when he did. He had done it a for a very long time, and though he had been terribly good at what he did, after a while one must lose his zest for doing it again and again. Artie Shaw is said to have quit performing because he couldn't bear having to play "Frenesi" one more time. In any event, Mitchell doesn't seem to have needed the money (Brendan Gill said his family was "wealthy"), and he took great pleasure in New York's amenities, including the Metropolitan Museum, the Grand Central Oyster Bar, and of course McSorley's alehouse.

What does seem odd is that a man with the memory of those Carolina Sundays in his bones should have found the New York of the middle third of the twentieth century the ideal subject for his civilized form of graveyard humor. But the New York emerging in the 1960s was not a city that lent itself to his particular "cast of mind." It needed writers who had grown up hearing the roar of the bullhorn, not the voice of Aunt Annie talking about the people down below.